"I am going…"

Reflections on the Last Words of the Saints

Mary Kathleen Glavich, SND

Illustrations by Christopher Santer

"I am going…"
Lessons from the Last Words of the Saints
by Mary Kathleen Glavich, SND

Edited by Patricia A. Lynch
Illustrations © 2017 Christopher Santer, www.pacemstudio.com
Cover design by Courter & Company

Scripture quotations are from the *New Revised Standard Version Bible*, copyright © 1989 by the Division of Christian Education of the National Council of the Churches of Christ in the USA. Used by permission.

Copyright © 2017 by Mary Kathleen Glavich, SND

Published by ACTA Publications, 4848 N. Clark St., Chicago, IL 60640, (800) 397-2282, www.actapublications.com

Library of Congress Catalog number: 2017950191
ISBN: 978-0-87946-595-7
Printed in the United States of America by Total Printing Systems
Year 30 29 28 27 26 25 24 23 22 21 20 19 18 17
Printing 15 14 13 12 11 10 9 8 7 6 5 4 3 2

♻ Text printed on 30% post-consumer recycled paper

Contents

Illustrations

Introduction

Dying words, especially those of heroes and other famous people, fascinate us. Some last words are common knowledge; we recall them as easily as our home address. Almost everyone knows, at least from Shakespeare, that as Julius Caesar passed from this life in 44 B.C., he asked, *"Et tu, Brute?"* And every student in the United States learns that, before his execution, American Revolutionary War hero Nathan Hale valiantly proclaimed, "I only regret that I have but one life to lose for my country." Recently, as Steve Jobs, cofounder and CEO of Apple, left this world, he looked past those gathered around his deathbed and mysteriously uttered, "Oh, wow! Oh, wow! Oh, wow!"

To us mortals, last words possess a kind of mystical significance. We deem them so important that we even allow condemned prisoners an opportunity to make a final statement. They may express remorse, anger, or gratitude to their families or wardens. They may apologize or steadfastly maintain innocence.

If you type *dying words* on an Internet search engine, you'll get pages and pages of hits, including the following gems.

- Just moments before receiving a fatal gunshot wound during the American Civil War, General John Sedgwick is reported to have remarked, "They couldn't hit an elephant at this distance."
- President Grover Cleveland wistfully said, "I have tried so hard to do the right."
- Some say comedian Lou Costello capped his fun-filled life by commenting, "That was the best ice-cream soda I ever tasted."
- According to his wife, Beatle George Harrison said, "Love one another."
- Leonardo da Vinci is said to confessed, "I have offended God and mankind because my work did not reach the quality it should have."

More meaningful for us than the last words of historical figures and celebrities are those of our loved ones. As they depart for the next life, they might assure us of their love, make a request, or impart some final advice. We tuck their dying words tenderly into our hearts.

Saints are our heroes and members of our family, our brothers and sisters in Christ. Because they serve as role models, it follows that their final words are both a legacy and challenge. As we move along our earthly journey, we treasure the words they uttered at their death and ponder their meaning for our own faith life.

Our greatest saint is Mary, the Mother of God. Unfortunately, we do not know her final words, but we do have the last words she spoke in the Gospel of John: "Do whatever he [Jesus] tells you." Now that's good advice. Nor do we have a record of the dying words of Joseph, Mary's husband. In fact, spoken words of Joseph on any topic are not recorded in any of the four gospels.

Other popular saints leave us without uttering their last thoughts. Saint Madeleine Sophie Barat, founder of the Society of the Sacred Heart, is one of these. Years before her death, she declared, "If God hears my prayers, there will be no last words of mine to repeat, for I shall say nothing at all." Her words were prophetic: Paralysis prevented her from speaking for the last days of her life. Another French saint, the beloved Saint John Vianney, known as the Curé of Ars, also died peacefully and silently in 1859. Perhaps humility kept his tongue in check. And although the great Saint Thomas Aquinas generated an avalanche of written words, apparently no one was able to record his final spoken words. You won't find Saint Benedict's last words in this book either, but his final gesture was a powerful statement. While standing in an oratory with arms uplifted in prayer after Communion, he died suddenly of a fever.

The dying words that have been preserved offer us a treasure trove for reflection. As we might expect, the majority of the saints died while uttering a prayer. Some humble saints, as holy as they were, still begged God for mercy. Many martyrs, in imitation of Jesus, forgave their enemies with their dying breath. Some saints delivered a final instruction to those surrounding their deathbed. And a few saints gifted with an irrepressible sense of humor and irony couldn't resist expiring with what might seem like a joke. Notable among this last group are the Roman deacon Saint Lawrence (page

136) and the English chancellor Saint Thomas More (page 206).

I was tempted to include the words of holy men and women like Blessed Miguel Pro. As this Jesuit faced the Mexican firing squad with his arms outstretched as if on a cross, he triumphantly proclaimed, "Long live Christ the king!" In the end I decided to focus solely on officially declared saints.

Each entry opens with a brief biography followed by the saint's last words, a reflection, and a suggestion for taking the saint's words to heart.

For those who would like to follow the liturgical calendar for the saints in this book, an index is provided on page 215.

We are unlikely to remember an event the same way as others. This is especially true in the case of a traumatic and emotional death. Our memories are colored by our relationship to the dying person and other factors. The same holds true for memories of the deaths of some saints. While most of the dying words quoted in this book have been authenticated, some might be the result of altered or embellished memory. And a few might reflect what someone *thought* the saint ought to have said! In any case, I hope you find these pages enlightening and inspiring.

It's doubtful that the saints planned their dying words. Rather, their final utterances were most likely spontaneous, just a few words flowing from the inspired wisdom of their entire lives. We usually don't think about our own death, much less our last words. What would you want your words to be as you exit this world and enter the next?

Mary Kathleen Glavich, SND

Note: The entry for each saint begins with the dates of birth and death, often approximate; titles; and feast day.

St.
Agatha

*Lord, my creator, you have protected me since
I was in the cradle. You have taken me from the love
of the world and given me patience to suffer.
Now receive my spirit.*

Saint Agatha

?–251 • Virgin, Martyr • February 5

Life

Saint Agatha, a Sicilian woman whose name means "good," lived during a time of Christian persecution. She died for her faith and for defending her purity. Legends of her martyrdom include some gruesome details. According to one legend, Agnes rebuffed the advances of the governor and was imprisoned in a brothel for a month. One night, after the governor had her breasts cut off, Saint Peter, martyred almost two centuries earlier, appeared in her cell and healed her. Then Agatha was rolled over hot coals and taken to prison where she died. A year later, when an eruption of Mt. Etna endangered the people in her home city of Catania, the people of the city prayed to her and the lava flow bypassed the city.

Last Words

Lord, my creator, you have protected me
since I was in the cradle.
You have taken me from the love of the world
and given me patience to suffer.
Now receive my spirit.

REFLECTION: A PERSONAL GOD

The Enlightenment, or Age of Reason, which evolved in the late seventeenth century, spawned Deism, or the Clockmaker God theory. This theory compared God to a person who makes a clock and then abandons it, letting it run by itself. Deists, including Benjamin Franklin, believed in God the Creator but did not think that he was involved at all in our lives. Saint Agatha's dying words reveal a belief diametrically opposed to this theory.

Agatha was truly "enlightened." God watched over her like a loving parent from the day she was born. She believed Jesus when he said, "Look at the birds of the air; they neither sow nor reap nor gather into barns, and yet your heavenly Father feeds them," and "If God so clothes the grass of the field....will he not much more clothe you?" (Matthew 6:26, 30). Agatha shared Saint Paul's view of God's intimate, all-encompassing presence: "In him we live and move and have our being" (Acts 17:28). She would also concur with Saint Catherine of Siena who said, "It seems to me that God has no other business than myself."

Convinced that God's fingerprints were all over her life, Agatha gave him credit in her last prayer for two of her extraordinary attributes: freedom from attachment to this world's pleasures and patience in enduring torments. Because she trusted that God's care extends beyond this present life, she asked him to receive her spirit. To Agatha, God was not a cold, distant being or force, but a loving Creator, a personal God who dotes on his human sons and daughters. She centered her life on God and loved him back so completely that she would accept no man as a husband, not even one of high rank. Steadfast in her convictions and commitment, Agatha sacrificed her life unconditionally.

RESPONSE

Sometimes the only explanation for unexpected, wonderful occurrences is the presence and action of our good God. Recall such times in your life and thank God for stepping in to help.

Saint Aloysius Gonzaga

1568–1591 • Confessor, Religious • June 21

LIFE

Saint Aloysius, an Italian aristocrat, was trained to be a soldier. During an illness, he read about the saints and was drawn to religious life, experiencing a revulsion to the violence and frivolous lifestyle of his culture. After serving as a page for the Spanish Infante Diego, he went against his father's wishes and joined the Jesuits. He relinquished his inheritance, made vows, received minor orders, and despite his poor health, practiced asceticism. While caring for plague victims in Rome, Aloysius contracted the disease. He died at age twenty-three, never having been ordained a priest.

LAST WORD

Jesus.

Reflection: The Name of Jesus

Saint Bernard of Clairvaux wrote that the name of Jesus is "honey in the mouth, melody in the ear, a cry of joy in the heart." Aloysius would have agreed emphatically. Jesus hemmed his life: Not only was Jesus his last word but it was reportedly his first!

According to the gospels, the angel Gabriel instructed Mary to name her child *Jesus*. Then, as if to insure that this was done, an angel repeated the instruction to Joseph. God the Father deliberately chose the name *Jesus* for his Son, giving as much thought to his child's name as human parents do. The name *Jesus* is derived from the Hebrew for "God saves." It expresses both the identity of Jesus as God and his world-changing mission: salvation.

Because Jesus is the name of the Son of God, it is the most holy and most powerful name. Saint Paul acknowledged this when he wrote that God gave Jesus "the name that is above every name, so that at the name of Jesus every knee should bend, in heaven and on earth and under the earth" (Philippians 2:9-10). Because Jesus is our savior, the one who died for us, his name is also precious, beloved.

No doubt, Saint Aloysius, who as a Jesuit was entirely devoted to Jesus, cringed each time the holy name was bandied about irreverently. Today is it not unusual to hear "Jesus" or "Christ" exclaimed in anger or surprise and to hear profanity in movies and online. How sad that God would have to order us in the second commandment to treat his name with respect.

A child once was asked to define *love*. "When someone loves you," she said, "the way they say your name is different. You know that your name is safe in their mouth." People who love God pronounce his name with awe and care because it stands for the almighty One who loved us first. The Church celebrates the Feast of the Holy Name of Jesus on January 3, just two days after the Solemnity of Mary, Mother of God.

Response

Do you dare point out to someone who habitually abuses the name of Jesus why you find it offensive? When you hear the holy name of Jesus used disrespectfully, counteract it at least by mentally praying, "Praised be Jesus Christ."

Saint André Bessette

1845–1937 • Religious • January 6

LIFE

Sickly and not very literate, Saint André was an unlikely prospect for the Congregation of the Holy Cross. However, his pastor sent him to this religious community with the note, "I'm sending you a saint." For forty years Brother André served as the doorkeeper at the College of Notre Dame in Montreal, Canada. Deep devotion to Saint Joseph compelled him to raise funds to build an oratory in his honor. This church became the Basilica of Saint Joseph's Oratory. A prayerful, holy man, André provided spiritual direction. Innumberable instances of miraculous healing have been attributed to his intercession. When he died, millions filed past his coffin.

LAST WORDS

Here is the grain.

Legend has it that the inventor of chess once showed the game to a king. When the king wanted to reward him, the wise man asked for what seemed a modest payment. He said, "On the first day give me one grain of wheat for the first square of the chessboard, on the second day two grains for the next square, four for the next, eight for the next, and so on for the sixty-four squares." The king agreed, and, amazingly, on the sixty-fourth day owed the man 18,446,744,073,709,551,615 grains!

This story of multiplication of grains is linked to André's life in three ways. First of all, God used one simple man, who could barely read or write, to do prodigious things and touch countless lives. Second, beginning in a small way by cutting boys' hair for a nickel, Brother André managed to accumulate enough funds to build a basilica. Third, the story involves grain, and the saint's last word was *grain*.

We might expect André to have died with the name Joseph on his lips. Instead he made the provocative statement, "Here is the grain." Most likely he was thinking of resurrection, for Jesus, referring to himself, taught, "Unless a grain of wheat falls into the earth and dies, it remains just a single grain; but if it dies, it bears much fruit" (John 12:24). Only if a grain dies and no longer exists as a grain can it burst forth with new life as a plant bearing many more grains. Saint Paul employed the same analogy to describe our death. He wrote, "What is sown is perishable, what is raised is imperishable. It is sown in dishonor, it is raised in glory. It is sown in weakness, it is raised in power. It is sown a physical body, it is raised a spiritual body" (1 Corinthians 15:42-44).

In his last words, Saint André manifested his faith in the divine Sower. He declared that he was ready to shed his life on earth and be reborn into new, eternal life. This is the life that Jesus won for us by undergoing death himself. Buried for three days, he rose from the earth ripe with glorified life and empowered to reproduce it in his followers a hundredfold.

RESPONSE

Multiply goodness. Perform a small, unexpected act of kindness for someone and ask him or her to pass it on.

Saint Andrew Kim Taegon

1821–1846 • Priest, Martyr • September 20

LIFE

Saint Andrew was born to Catholic converts in Korea. During a persecution of Christians, his father, a farmer, was martyred. Andrew attended a seminary in Macao, China, and was ordained in Shanghai, becoming the first Korean-born priest. He returned to Korea and ministered secretly, sneaking missionaries into the country. He was arrested, tortured, and beheaded near what is now Seoul. Andrew was canonized with 102 other Korean martyrs.

LAST WORDS

My immortal life is on the point of beginning.
Become Christians if you wish to be happy after death,
because God has eternal chastisements in store
for those who have refused to know him.

REFLECTION: PORTRAIT OF A CHRISTIAN

The grace of being a baptized Christian has not been an option for everyone. Only people living during the past two thousand years have been favored this way, and today only about one-third of the world's population is Christian. For some reason, God gave us Catholics the privilege of being born when and where Christianity exists. Perhaps our parents handed on their faith to us, or some encounter or experience sparked our faith in Jesus Christ.

Saint Andrew inherited the faith at a dangerous time when Christianity was banned in his country. He was such a committed Christian that he became a priest and, soon after, a martyr. In his final testimony he said that those who accept Christ will be happy *after* death, but Christians are also happy *before* death. They take comfort in knowing that the universe rests in the hands of a wise, benevolent God. They bask in the belief that God loves us with such a crazy love that he became one of us. God not only forgives sins and failings but atoned for them in our stead by embracing suffering and death.

Christians are not burdened by guilty consciences but find relief in the Sacrament of Penance. They enjoy life fully and are grateful for every moment and every thing. When faced with challenges and hardships, they know they can turn to God and be heard. They are convinced that God cares for them as individuals and intends for them to live forever in his company. Christians possess the gift of hearing God speak to their hearts in Scripture. Their lives have inherent meaning and amazing purpose. Belief in Jesus fill Christians with hope. Finally, the abyss of death does not frighten Christians; for them death leads not to annihilation or everlasting punishment, but to eternal life.

RESPONSE

On a scale from one to ten, how would you rate the state of your Christian life? Is it full strength or diluted? Explain. Take some steps to become a better Christian.

Saint Angela Merici

1474–1540 • Virgin, Religious, Founder • January 27

LIFE

Saint Angela was born in Italy and orphaned at age fifteen. She then lived with her uncle and joined the Third Order of Saint Francis. Convinced that Christian education for girls led to Christian families, she returned to her town at age twenty and began to teach girls in her home. Next she opened a school in a nearby town. Then with twelve young women, she started the Company of Saint Ursula, a secular institute. Although the women took no vows, they practiced poverty, chastity, and obedience. They lived in their own homes and did not wear a habit. Angela's association developed into the religious community known as the Ursulines.

LAST WORDS

Jesus, Jesus. Into your hands I commend my spirit.

Reflection: Spreading the Name of Jesus

I once visited El Salvador armed with a smattering of Spanish. One day a young man sitting on a porch with me asked how many children I had. Not knowing the Spanish term for religious sister, I replied that I was married to Jesus. A few seconds later, another young man joined us and I asked his name. "Jesus," he said.

The name *Jesus* is as popular in many cultures today as it was in the time of Jesus. However, Jesus as the name of the Son of God is unique. When the apostle Peter was hauled out of prison and made to stand before the high priest and others, he declared, "There is no other name under heaven given among mortals by which we must be saved" (Acts 4:12). Saint Angela was wise to repeat this name in the moments before her eternal fate was decided. Fortuitously, her feast day lands in January, the month dedicated to the Holy Name of Jesus.

Angela spent her life trying to make Jesus known and loved by educating future mothers. In our era of globalization and social media, we have the potential to make his holy name known to the ends of the earth. We can educate people not only in our Catholic institutions but via the radio, television, the written word, and, of course, the Internet.

Out of reverence, Jewish people have always refrained from speaking and writing the name of God. On the other hand, we who know and love Jesus as God wrapped in flesh pronounce his name over and over. We say it in prayer and in attempts to stir others to begin or deepen a relationship with him. And we anticipate the day when we will finally hear him say our name.

Response

Place a card or paper with the name of Jesus where you will see it often and be reminded to think of him. Sing or listen to a hymn that contains the name of Jesus.

Saint Anselm

1033–1109 • Abbot, Archbishop, Doctor of the Church • April 21

LIFE

Born into a noble family in Burgundy, Saint Anselm joined a Benedictine monastery in France. After becoming its abbot, he was appointed Archbishop of Canterbury. Caught in a power struggle between the papacy and the kingdom, Anselm was exiled twice. A philosopher and theologian, he adopted the motto "faith seeking understanding." His writings draw on reason to explore doctrines such as the existence of God, creation, the Trinity, and atonement. Anselm's teachings influenced the thinking of later theologians and helped shape what we believe today.

LAST WORDS

I shall gladly obey his call;
yet I should also feel grateful
if he would grant me a little longer time with you,
and if I could be permitted to solve a question—
the origin of the soul.

REFLECTION: GROWING IN KNOWLEDGE OF GOD

A prayer by Saint Catherine of Siena includes this line: "O Eternal Trinity, you are as deep a mystery as the sea, in whom the more I seek, the more I find; and the more I find, the more I seek." Anselm was driven to plumb the depths of God by applying his great intellect to the doctrines of the Church. Even as he lay dying, he desired to delve into one more topic.

We are curious creatures. We have an innate desire to know truth. We launch rockets and satellites to discover more about space. We excavate archeological sites and venture into caves to learn more about our beginnings on earth. We use deep-sea submersibles to explore the mysteries of the ocean. In countless laboratories we carry out research to broaden our understanding of our world.

Most of us are acquainted with the basic teachings of the Church. However, the two-thousand-year body of knowledge related to God, the Church, and life is vast. We can always learn more. Some mysteries we will never fully grasp.

Among the tools for educating ourselves about the faith, we have, first and foremost, *The Catechism of the Catholic Church*. We also have papal encyclicals, religious books, magazines, newspapers, and DVDs. The Internet offers websites devoted to Catholic teachings for adults and children. Courses, lectures, missions, and retreats are other opportunities for deepening our knowledge of the faith. Hopefully our craving for knowledge will be satisfied at the end of all our searching as was Saint Anselm's when he beheld ultimate Truth.

RESPONSE

Fight religious illiteracy. Read a book about some aspect of the faith and pass the book on to others.

Saint Anthony Daniels

1601–1648 • Priest, Religious, Martyr • October 19

LIFE

Saint Anthony, a French Jesuit, became a missionary to the Huron Indians in Canada. One day the Iroquois attacked while the Huron elders, women, and children were gathered in the chapel. Anthony ordered the Huron people to leave and save themselves. Those words were his last. Then he courageously tried to divert the attackers by walking toward them while holding up a cross. The fatal gunshot Anthony received made him one of the eight North American martyrs.

LAST WORDS

I will stay here. We will meet in heaven.

Reflection: Heaven

Our faith in heaven is not just wishful thinking. No, it is solidly founded on Jesus' promise of eternal life. In his Last Supper farewell to his apostles, Jesus told of the many dwelling places in his Father's house. Like a homeowner expecting guests, he was going to get one ready for them. (See John 14:2.) We don't know any more than that from the gospels. What heaven is like remains a well-kept secret. According to Scripture, Saint Paul was favored with a vision of heaven, but he gave no clue as to what he beheld except to say that it was indescribable. He explained that what God has prepared for those who love him was something "no eye has seen, nor ear heard, nor the human heart conceived" (1 Corinthians 2:9).

We can, however, draw conclusions about heaven from this present life. Sometimes our world is so exquisitely beautiful that it brings tears to our eyes. Imagine, then, how glorious heaven, the dwelling place of God, the architect of the universe, must be! Furthermore, consider the happiness that sometimes bubbles up in us, especially when we know we are loved. This is but an inkling of the sweet joy that will be ours in heaven. There we will be loved completely and without end by the supreme Lover.

There is another reason for this heavenly joy. In the convent we have a saying, "It's not the house you live in but the cows you live with that make the difference." In heaven not only will we be living with our Maker, our Savior, and our best Friend, the only one able to satisfy the gnawing longing in our hearts, but our companions will be the Blessed Virgin Mary, our mother; hosts of angels; and all the other saints—our favorites and some who may surprise us. We will also be reunited with our deceased loved ones. Heaven will be one fantastic party from which no one ever has to go home.

Because of our faith in the risen Christ, we can repeat Saint Anthony's words and assure those who are dying, "We will meet in heaven." Whom do you look forward to seeing in the next world?

Response

Take action to help others hear the good news about Jesus and the kingdom of heaven. Serve as an "armchair missionary" by donating to the missions, saying a prayer for missionaries, or "adopting" a missionary from your diocese.

Saint Anthony of Egypt

251–356 • Abbot, Desert Father • January 17

LIFE

Saint Anthony was the son of wealthy Egyptian landowners who died when he was only twenty years old. After their deaths, he divested himself of his property and possessions and left home to live in the silence and solitude of the desert. A hermit there taught him how to pray and do penance. Soon Anthony's holiness attracted others. After founding a monastery for hermits and with hopes of martyrdom, he left the desert to minister to persecuted Christians in prison. After that he returned to the desert, only to leave again to preach against Arianism, a heresy that denied the divinity of Christ. Anthony finally left this earth for heaven at the age of 105.

LAST WORDS

Farewell, my children.
Anthony is departing
and will no longer be with you.

Reflection: Positive Peer Pressure

I can claim as my spiritual children the hundreds of students who sat in my religion classes. Today people who are nurtured by my writing and speaking can also be numbered among my "offspring." This is the sense with which Saint Anthony used the word *children* as he said goodbye to the people he had formed in the faith. He did not give them physical life, but in a very real way he gave birth to and nurtured their spiritual life. His followers did not inherit his genes, but they took on his faith and his asceticism.

Anthony made a permanent impression on the spiritual children he was leaving behind. Like a parent, he taught them values and fostered virtues. He served as a positive role model. With Saint Paul, he could say, "Be imitators of me, as I am of Christ" (1 Corinthians 11:1). Anthony truly deserves the title "desert father."

We human beings are mimics. Did you ever notice what happens when people stand talking together? Before long they are all holding their arms the same way. The fashion industry depends on our desire to be like others. We, too, influence people whose lives we touch, whether or not we or they realize it. People absorb our attitudes and our thoughts. They might even imitate the way we speak or walk. To some degree our words and actions help form every person we meet face-to-face or through social media. We can nudge people to be saints or sinners. What kind of "children" are you raising?

Response

Find a way to mentor someone. You might become a volunteer tutor, join a support group, teach someone a skill, or share your faith with a younger person or a neighbor.

Saint Anthony of Padua

1195–1231 • Priest, Religious, Doctor of the Church • June 13

LIFE

Born in Lisbon, Portugal, Saint Anthony joined the Augustinian order. After seeing the bodies of five Franciscans martyred in Morocco, he left the Augustinians and joined the Franciscans. He went to Morocco, but had to leave due to ill health. On the way home a storm redirected his ship to Italy where he remained for some time. Then one day he gave a spontaneous homily which revealed his remarkable gift for preaching. He then traveled throughout Italy, France, and Belgium, preaching and, in effect, converting many heretics. One incident in the life of the saint explains a popular prayer practice. Legend has it that a novice ran off with the saint's precious annotated Psalter. Later the novice returned with the stolen book. For centuries thereafter, the faithful have turned to Anthony for help in locating lost objects. Have you?

LAST WORDS

I see my Lord.

Reflection: The Physical Appearance of Jesus

A prostitute who had turned her life around became involved in our parish. She claimed to have visions of Jesus. We non-visionaries can only speculate about what Jesus looked like, but because he was a first-century Jewish man, we can surmise that he was about 5'4" and olive-skinned with black or brown hair and brown eyes. It's debatable whether Jesus had a beard or long hair. The Shroud of Turin, not yet proven to be authentic, supports the possibility that he had both.

Some people assume that because Jesus was the Son of God, he was strikingly handsome, like King David who, according to Scripture, was good-looking and had beautiful eyes. (See 1 Samuel 16:12.) Others, though, quote the prophet Isaiah who states, "He had no form or majesty that we should look at him, nothing in his appearance that we should desire him" (Isaiah 53:2). As a construction worker, Jesus most likely was strong and muscular. As an itinerant preacher who lived outdoors and trekked for miles, sometimes through deserts, he must have been tough and tanned. Because Jesus addressed crowds of thousands without a microphone, he surely had a booming voice. Without question Jesus greatly resembled his mother, Mary of Nazareth.

Regardless of his physical appearance, Jesus possessed a charisma that drew people to him like a magnet. The apostles, early martyrs, and, centuries later, Saint Anthony addressed him as "my Lord" and devoted their lives to him. Millions still follow him.

We might wish that we had lived in Galilee when Jesus did so we could meet him in the flesh and hear his voice as did his first disciples. Most saints had the same desire. Like them, we must wait until we die to see Jesus face-to-face and enjoy the Beatific Vision. In the meantime, our love is literally blind. However, we can count on the last beatitude of Jesus, "Blessed are those who have not seen and yet have come to believe" (John 20:29).

Response

Imagine that Jesus, the risen Lord, stands before you, smiling and gazing on you with love. What would you say to him? Jesus is with you now, though invisible. Speak to him.

Saint Antonius of Florence

1389–1459 • Bishop, Religious • May 2

LIFE

When Saint Antonius, an only child, was a thin, sickly fifteen-year-old, he petitioned to become a Dominican. His rejection was subtle: The religious superiors in that order asked him to return once he had memorized canon law. He did just that! Thus Antonius became a Dominican priest, a theologian, and a participant in the Council of Florence. Against his wishes, he was appointed Archbishop of Florence. Antonius worked for reform in his community and in the Church and is known for his writings. His last words were an oft-recited religious maxim.

LAST WORDS

To serve God is to reign.

In a beloved fairy tale, Cinderella is magically transformed from a scorned family servant into a princess. This is the trajectory of Jesus' life. Philippians 2:5-11, thought to be an early Christian hymn, is a biography of Jesus in a nutshell. The first half describes how he humbled himself and became a slave. The second half joyously proclaims that because Jesus stooped to serve, God exalted him. Jesus Christ is Lord.

Of course, the most striking way Jesus served was by dying and rising to procure our eternal happiness. But during his time on earth, he often assumed the role of servant *par excellence*. Jesus tirelessly taught about God and explained how to live a good life. Tapping into his divine power, Jesus healed droves of sick people and filled the stomachs of hungry people. He brought sinners peace by offering forgiveness. Several times he helped frustrated fishermen fill their nets. One of his last deeds on earth was washing the feet of his apostles, a shocking, revolutionary lesson on rendering loving service.

Through Scripture, God urges us to imitate the service of Jesus, to put others' interests ahead of our own. Ultimately, by serving others, we serve God. We are his arms and legs, conveying his love to others. Some servants are esteemed as heroes. Think of Saint Teresa of Calcutta, Mahatma Gandhi, Martin Luther King, Jr., firefighters, police officers, and those who serve in the armed forces. The unrecognized and unsung heroes, however, number in the billions. An essay contest required students to answer the question "Who is your hero?" Most teens replied, "Mom." Parents serve their families day in and day out, sometimes in heroic ways.

Pope Saint Gregory I was the first pope to adopt for himself the title "Servant of the Servants of God." Actually this title should fit any Christian as perfectly as the glass slipper fit Cinderella. If we think of ourselves as servants and act accordingly, we will be crowned with everlasting glory in God's kingdom and reign with him. We will live happily ever after.

RESPONSE

Try to serve people today in a way that will surprise them and bring them joy. Or thank someone who has served you and rarely is shown appreciation.

Saint Bede the Venerable

c. 672–735 • Priest, Religious, Doctor of the Church • May 25

LIFE

Born in England, Saint Bede became a Benedictine monk and devoted his life to prayer, writing, and teaching. The majority of his books were on Scripture, but he is most remembered for his *Ecclesiastical History of the English People*. Bede's life was not marked by miracles, visions, or other extraordinary events. He attained sanctity by living simply and well. He uttered his last words as he was beginning to sing his favorite prayer.

LAST WORDS

Glory be to the Father, and to the Son, and to the Holy Spirit.

Reflection: Glorifying God with Our Lives

In a preschool religion class, Gloria worked intently on coloring a picture, all the while repeating the refrain from "Angels We Have Heard on High" in her sweet voice: "Glo-o-o-o-ria, in excelsis Deo." This carol may have been her favorite because it contained her name, or she may simply have been praising God.

Saint Bede closed his life with a grand finale, glorifying the Trinity in song as he would for eternity in heaven. After all, he was—we *all* were—created to praise God. So were the angels. Their job description has worshiping God at the top of the list. Giving glory to God is logical and right, for God is the supreme being, almighty, all-knowing, and a perfect ten in every category. The Trinity is the wellspring of our being, maintains our existence, promises unending joy, and dwells in us as a life coach. Besides praise, we owe our creator, redeemer, and sanctifier profound gratitude.

Saint Irenaeus explained that the glory of God is a human being fully alive. Being fully alive means striving to be the best persons we can be and using the gifts God has given us: singing if we are blessed with a fine voice, acting if we have a flair for acting, and crafting things if we are good with our hands. As the saying goes, "It is better to wear out than to rust out." When we are fully alive, we live with passion. We are awake to the beauty of the world. We thrive on working, talking, playing, and laughing with others. And we reflect deeply on our experiences and the meaning of life.

Bede was fully alive, making his whole life a symphony of praise. He prayed and made use of his talents for writing and teaching. He also loved his fellow monks, presenting each of them with a gift from his deathbed.

One option for the Rite of Dismissal at Mass is "Go in peace and glorify God with your lives." We heed that command by loving God and others, by doing ordinary and extraordinarily things as well as possible, and by not letting the gifts God has showered on us go to waste. Whatever we do, it will never be enough.

Response

What in creation do you especially treasure? Is there a beautiful place, a certain person, or a talent you or someone else possesses? Give God glory for that treasure—in song if you can.

Saint Benildus

1805–1862 • Religious • August 13

LIFE

Pierre Romançon, born in France, joined the Christian Brothers when he was only fourteen. Even at that young age he was called upon to serve as a substitute teacher. As Brother Benildus, he spent forty-one years teaching religion and other subjects. Benildus is thought to have inspired the vocations of at least twenty students. When Benildus was canonized, Pope Paul VI explained that he had attained sanctity by enduring "the terrible daily grind."

LAST WORDS

How happy one is to die in our holy state.

Reflection: A Religious Vocation

Once a year on the World Day of Prayer for Vocations, the Church shines a spotlight on religious vocations. For a number of reasons, the number of priests and consecrated religious in the United States is in decline. For example, some Catholics may think that religious life seems like as a prison sentence. Saint Benildus would have been the first to disagree.

When his father pressured him to leave the Christian Brothers, Benildus exclaimed, "If I had to live here on nothing but potato skins, I would not leave this house!" Benildus thrived in religious life. He was convinced that God's dream for him was to be a brother. This path was how he could best serve God and others and be fulfilled.

All of us have the primary vocation to be holy, to mirror God's love. We carry out this vocation in a particular state of life. It's as if we're all on a highway to heaven, but in different lanes. Most travel in the lane of marriage, assisting a spouse and children to become saints. Rarer are those in the lane of religious life, handing over their entire lives to God and God's people. Free from family responsibilities, they have more time to devote to prayer and works of charity. Ordinarily they take vows of poverty, chastity, and obedience in order to more closely follow in the footsteps of Jesus. Also, most religious live in community, supported by like-minded companions.

To people obsessed with wealth, sex, fame, or power, a religious life looks foolish—a waste of life. But, as Jesus asked, what good is it to gain the whole world and lose your soul? (See Mark 8:36.) Persons God calls to save their souls as a brother or sister religious will only be truly happy by responding wholeheartedly. Similarly, persons who in God's plan are to be ordained, married, or single will achieve happiness here and hereafter by being faithful to their calls. No matter the lane we travel, we encounter potholes, detours, and some stretches of boring scenery. Benildus taught us that victory lies in performing common things in an uncommon way.

Response

Pray that God invites more people to religious life and that they have the courage and wisdom to RSVP with a yes. If you know someone who has potential for religious life, suggest that he or she consider it.

St. Bernadette

Holy Mary, Mother of God,
pray for me, a poor sinner, a poor sinner.

Saint Bernadette

1844–1879 • Virgin, Religious • April 16

LIFE

Saint Bernadette was the oldest of five children in a destitute French family. She suffered from asthma and other ailments and had difficulty learning the catechism. Yet, at age fourteen she was favored with the first of eighteen visions of the Blessed Virgin Mary, who identified herself as the Immaculate Conception. Mary asked that a chapel be built at the site of her visions. Today millions visit the Shrine of Our Lady of Lourdes, many hoping for a cure through its healing waters. Bernadette became a humble sister who worked in the convent infirmary and sacristy until she died of tuberculosis.

LAST WORDS

Holy Mary, Mother of God,
pray for me, a poor sinner, a poor sinner.

Reflection: Mary, Refuge of Sinners

After a pilgrimage to Lourdes, a priest presented his young nephew with a statue of Mary. The boy placed the image of Mary next to his bed and declared that she would protect him. "From what?" asked the uncle. "From monsters," the boy replied.

Just as the boy counted on Mary for protection, Saint Bernadette invoked the help of the Mother of God at the frightening hour of her death. It's no surprise that she did so. After all, Bernadette knew Our Lady personally and had witnessed her motherly concern for us. The Blessed Virgin visited Lourdes in order to establish a place of healing for the sick and to remind us to do penance and pray for sinners. She showed that she has a mother's heart for us, the brothers and sisters of her divine son.

What may be puzzling, though, is that the saint called herself a poor sinner. What sins did Bernadette ever have to confess in her short life? She had been a good, obedient child and had been kind to her siblings. After the miraculous encounters, she shunned publicity and took refuge in a convent. There she lived in self-effacement, saying, "What does one do with a broom when one has finished sweeping? Why, put it in the corner." Perhaps Bernadette described herself as a poor sinner because, having beheld Mary, a woman who was sinless since her conception, she realized that by comparison she was a sinner, tainted by original and personal sin.

Like Bernadette, we can look to our heavenly mother Mary when we are dying. She ushered her husband and her son into the next life. She will also be with us. Each time we pray the Hail Mary we ask her to pray for us at the hour of our death. When we pray the rosary, as Bernadette did during Mary's visits, we ask this fifty-three times! Good mother that Mary is, she will not refuse us.

Response

What virtue do you most admire in Mary? Ask your heavenly mother to pray that you have the grace to practice that virtue in your own life. Right now pray a Hail Mary slowly and thoughtfully.

Saint Boniface

672–754 • Monk, Bishop, Martyr • June 5

Life

Born in England as Winfrid, Saint Boniface is known today as the Apostle to Germany. Entering the Benedictines, he answered the call to be a missionary in Holland, a country whose ruler had declared war on Christians, and then asked Pope Gregory II where he could serve next. After changing his name to Boniface, a name meaning "doer of good deeds," the pope sent him to Germany, where Boniface and his followers founded or renewed many dioceses. After the pope made him a bishop, he returned to Holland. One day as Boniface prepared to celebrate Confirmation, he and about fifty converts were murdered by pagans. His last words were addressed to those facing martyrdom with him.

Last Words

That moment of freedom
we have yearned for is right here.
So be heroic in the Lord
and suffer this royal grace of his will gladly.
Keep your trust in him
and he will set your souls free.

Reflection: Martyrdom

Almost everyone would agree with the words of poet Dylan Thomas: "Do not go gentle into that good night" but "rage against the dying of the light." Saint Boniface took the opposite stance toward death: He welcomed it. His longing for martyrdom may seem unnatural because it contradicts the strong drive for self-preservation, but he saw dying as a "moment of freedom," an outlook shaped by Scripture and Christian theology.

Boniface defined death as a release from the devastating punishment of being separated from our good and loving Creator. What's more, Boniface called martyrdom a "royal grace," in other words, a privilege or favor. We believe that a Christian who is killed for the faith goes directly to heaven. In light of this belief, early Christians honored the martyrs as saints from the beginning and prayed at their tombs. Even today the canonization of a martyr does not require the usual number of miracles. The very act of dying for the faith is ample confirmation of sainthood.

A person facing martyrdom surely needs an unfailing trust in God. This trust is built up day by day by praying and by practicing the faith. Models like Boniface bolster our commitment to Jesus. They illustrate that, with the help of God's grace, it is possible to think and live in a way that supercedes what is natural. The martyrs go down in history not as fools for surrendering their lives, but as heroes for standing firm for their faith.

Response

In what countries are Christians being persecuted and killed today? Pray and do penance that the persecuted may hold onto the faith and that persecutions will cease.

Saint Bruno

c. 1030–1101 • Priest, Hermit, Founder • October 6

Life

Saint Bruno, born in Germany, was ordained a priest and became a renowned theology teacher and preacher in Rheims, France. After he criticized an archbishop for paying for his position in the Church, the archbishop was removed. In consequence, Bruno's property was stolen. Bruno and six companions decided to live as hermits, choosing the mountains of Chartreuse, France, as the location for their chapel. Six years later, Pope Urban II, a former student of Bruno, summoned him to Rome to serve as his advisor. Humbly refusing to be named a bishop, Bruno established another hermitage in Italy. He is remembered as the founder of the Carthusian monks.

Last Words

I believe that the sacred bread and wine of the Eucharist is Jesus Christ, body and blood, soul and divinity.

Reflection: The Eucharist

When Saint Bruno was dying, he recited the Creed and then affirmed his belief in the Eucharist as the body and blood of Jesus. Catholics believe something incredible: that bread and wine become God. That is the depth of God's love for us. Love does foolish things. How often people say, "I love you so much I could eat you up." God literally lets us "eat him up." By becoming our food and drink, God becomes one with us, closer than anyone else could ever be. Each Mass is a celebration of the union of divinity and humanity.

Our faith in the Eucharist is grounded in Scripture and Tradition. At his last supper, Jesus took bread and said, "This is my body." Then he passed a cup of wine and stated, "This is my blood." Some faith traditions hold that these words were symbolic. But then how do you explain what Jesus declared the day he foretold the Eucharist? "Those who eat my flesh and drink my blood have eternal life…for my flesh is true food and my blood is true drink" (John 6:54-55). The Jews, whose kosher laws require that blood be drained from meat, were appalled by what sounded like cannibalism. Even though many no longer followed him, Jesus didn't recant or even soften his words. He really meant them.

The Eucharist is shared all over the globe, day after day. For some two thousand years, Catholics have taken the words of Jesus at face value. Still, how easily we let our reception of the Eucharist become routine and stale, forgetting what an astounding miracle it is. We might even fail to take advantage of this gift. As Saint Augustine wistfully noted, "Christ is the bread, awaiting hunger."

After Bruno died, he was welcomed into the eternal banquet by the "Living Bread" himself.

Response

What prayers do you offer after receiving Communion? Plan your words to the risen Lord ahead of time so that they may better express all the love and gratitude he deserves.

Saint Catherine of Siena

1347–1380 • Virgin, Doctor of the Church, Mystic • April 29

LIFE

Saint Catherine was the twenty-third child of a cloth dyer and his wife from Siena, Italy. Rejecting both marriage and the convent, she joined the Third Order of St. Dominic at age sixteen. While living at home, she led a life of solitude, prayer, and penance until Jesus called her to go out in public. From then on she served the poor, became a spiritual guide, and traveled throughout Italy, preaching, writing spiritual works, and acting as a peacemaker. She even persuaded Pope Gregory XI to return the seat of the papacy from Avignon to Rome. Catherine was favored with visions, a mystical marriage with Christ, and the stigmata.

LAST WORDS

Blood! Blood!

REFLECTION: THE PRECIOUS BLOOD

Walking down a dark hall in an unfamiliar convent, I came upon a gruesome pietà. It depicted the body of Jesus striped with gashes and covered with blood. Accustomed to our sanitized crucifixes, I found this realistic statue shocking yet thought provoking. It forcibly brought home the fact that Jesus shed his blood for us. By undergoing a brutal, ignominious death on a cross, he irrefutably demonstrated his love and mercy. Jesus rescued all humankind from eternal death. As his sacred blood streamed down and soaked the earth, it birthed a new creation.

Saint Catherine's spirituality was dominated by two themes: the blood of Christ and the Eucharist. Some of her expressions about the Precious Blood may strike us as strange and extreme. For example, she spoke of bathing ourselves in this blood and being inebriated with it.

Catherine's focus on blood is reminiscent of Jewish religious practices. In the centuries before the sacrifice of Calvary, sacrifices of adoration or atonement involved the blood of ritually slaughtered animals. For example, God's covenant was sealed when Moses sprinkled the blood of calves and goats on the Hebrew people. Animals were sacrificed daily at the Temple in Jerusalem, but the sacrifice of Jesus replaced all sacrifices. In shedding his blood, Jesus, the God-Man, gave birth to eternal life and established a new covenant. At every Eucharist, just as two people mingle their blood to become blood brothers, the Eucharistic blood of Jesus unites with ours.

According to Scripture, saints like Catherine wear heavenly white robes washed in the blood of the Lamb. (See Revelation 7:14.) Likewise, our baptismal robes are white, symbolizing that the blood of Christ has purified us from sin and given us a share in his glory.

RESPONSE

Pray the Litany of the Precious Blood found on page 215. Then spend some time gazing at a crucifix and pondering God's immense love for you.

Saint Charbel Makhlouf

1828–1898 • Monk, Priest, Hermit • July 24

Life

Saint Charbel, born in Lebanon, was a member of the Maronite Church, an Eastern Rite Catholic Church. He entered religious life as a monk at the Monastery of Saint Maron and later was ordained a priest. After moving to a nearby hermitage and living alone in silence, prayer, and asceticism, he gained a reputation for holiness. One day while celebrating Mass, he suffered a stroke during the consecration. For the next eight days until his death on Christmas Eve, he repeated the Father of Truth prayer from the Maronite Rite Holy Liturgy. Charbel's life was marked by miracles during his time on earth and after his death.

Last Words

Father of Truth, behold your Son,
a sacrifice pleasing to you.
Accept this offering of him who died for me.

Reflection: Self-denial

Actor Christian Bale lost fifty-four pounds to play an emaciated man in the movie *The Machinist*. A year later, he had bulked up enough for the role of a muscular Batman. Dancers, athletes, and actors go to great lengths getting their bodies in shape to reach their goals. They follow strict diets and undertake rigorous workout routines. Their self-denial and sacrifices are for secular reasons, but Saint Charbel practiced harsh penances as a strategy for a spiritual reason: to grow in virtue. He slept on a straw mattress with a board for a pillow, wore a hair shirt, ate one meal a day, and sacrificed ordinary pleasures. In doing so, he resembled Jesus, who emptied himself to become man and sacrificed himself for the salvation of humankind.

Just as a good workout tones our muscles, self-denial builds our strength for spiritual combat. It can also serve as a form of penance. Keep in mind that the form of fasting that God urges is to loose the chains of injustice and to let the oppressed go free. (See Isaiah 58:6.) This means making God and others, not ourselves, the center of our lives. With a little self-denial added to our daily routine, our physical life and spiritual life will flourish.

Response

How do your daily life and work require self-denial? Make some sacrifice today that will be pleasing to God. Fast from something you enjoy or take action on behalf of those who are suffering.

Saint Charles Borromeo

1538–1584 • Bishop • November 4

LIFE

At age twenty-one, Italian-born Saint Charles already had earned
doctorates in civil and canon law when his uncle Pope Pius IV made
him cardinal and administrator of Milan, Italy. As secretary of state
at the Vatican, he assisted with the Council of Trent. and helped reform Rome. As archbishop of Milan, he was devoted to his diocese.
He established orphanages, hospitals, homes for neglected women,
seminaries, and colleges, and worked to reform the priesthood and
religious life. When a famine and plague struck, Charles cared for
his people and used his own fortune to provide food for them. He
is the patron of seminaries.

LAST WORDS

Behold I come. Your will be done.

Reflection: Responding to God's Call

When I entered the convent, it was the custom to ring a bell over the public address system to summon us to prayer. We were to stop working immediately and head straight to chapel. Any sister who came late had to kneel in the middle aisle, red-faced, until the superior decided to give her the signal to go to her pew.

Saint Charles never needed a practice like this. He possessed the self-discipline to answer any call promptly, especially if the call came from God. That is why at the age of forty-six, when there was still so much work for him to do, Charles dropped everything and departed this life. His last words are those of a faithful servant, echoing the words of Jesus in the Garden of Gethsemane. Both Jesus and Charles surrendered themselves to whatever God wished, certain that it would be for the good.

We don't know how many days we have left to us on earth. Young people may think they are immortal, but we learn that no one lives forever. For example, we pray, "The days of our life are seventy years, or perhaps eighty, if we are strong" (Psalm 90:10). Each day is a gift to fill as we wish. Another Charles, Blessed Charles de Foucauld, greeted each morning with the prayer, "Lord, one more day to love you!" Doubtless, this is how Charles Borromeo welcomed each day. Then, judging from his numerous accomplishments, he filled the rest of the day with whatever business God asked of him.

When our time is up and we are called home, may we children of God not hesitate, but run rejoicing to our Father, saying, "Coming!"

Response

God calls us through the words of other people, our experiences, and inspirations that flash across our minds. Be quiet and listen for what God is calling you to today.

Saint Charles Lwanga

1860 or 1865–1886 • Martyr • June 3

LIFE

Saint Charles was a court page under Mkasa, a Christian and the master of pages for King Mwanga of Uganda, a brutal ruler who persecuted Christians. Charles was baptized on the day Mkasa was killed for criticizing the king's immoral sexual acts. When Charles replaced Mkasa as head of pages, he urged them not to participate in the king's licentious conduct. Enraged, King Mwanga sentenced him and twenty-one young Christian pages to death. Tightly bound, they were marched thirty-seven miles to the place of execution. They prayed and sang as they awaited their martyrdom and then were burned alive.

LAST WORDS

You are burning me, but it is as if you were pouring water over my body. Katonda (my God)!

Reflection: Desperation

On the cross, Jesus cried out, quoting Psalm 22: "My God, my God, why have you forsaken me?" This puzzling cry of anguish has been interpreted in several ways. The fact that the long psalm ends on a hopeful note implies that Jesus may have been anticipating his victory on Easter Sunday. And since this psalm foretells the coming of the Savior, Jesus might have used it to identify himself as the messiah. On the other hand, the words signal that Jesus was truly one with human beings. We too may think God has deserted us in times when we find ourselves swallowed up by a frightening darkness.

Like Jesus, Saint Charles experienced an excruciating, terrifying death as a result of obeying his God. And he called on God with his last breath, pleading for strength and comfort from the all-powerful One who created him.

Pope Francis endorsed the prayers of lamentation found in many other psalms and prayers besides Psalm 22, recommending we pray to God as a friend, speaking frankly, arguing, if necessary, and demanding action. When we are in the clutches of pain and suffering, we can call on God who knows what it is to suffer. Jesus promised over and over again that God, the most solicitous of all fathers, would answer our prayers. In any tragedy that befalls us—the death of a loved one, a car accident, the loss of a job, or a devastating diagnosis—we can immediately run for refuge to the God who loves us.

Response

Write your own prayer of lamentation for something that is happening in your life right now or for a past experience.

Saint Chi Zhuze

1882–1900 • Catechumen, Martyr • July 9

LIFE

At age seventeen, Saint Chi Zhuze, born in China, was attracted to the Catholic faith and began attending Mass. During the Boxer Rebellion at the turn of the twentieth century, Chi's family expelled him because he would not worship idols. A Catholic man gave Chi refuge and hired him as a servant, but when the persecution of Catholics increased, Chi's parents ordered him home. On the way, Boxers met him and demanded that he worship idols. Chi refused, identifying himself as a Catholic. The Boxers cut off his arm before flaying him alive. His last words were spoken after his arm was removed. In time, Chi's parents converted to Catholicism.

LAST WORDS

Every piece of my flesh, every drop of my blood, will tell you that I am Christian.

Reflection: True-blue Christians

Part-time Christians or Christians in name only could be characterized as laughing in the face of God. Saint Chi was a *full-time* Christian, proving it in word and deed by his life and his death. We might not be asked to surrender our lives for our faith, but we can spend them in such a way that it's obvious to our families, neighbors, and co-workers that we follow Jesus. Our faith ought to shine out like the beacon of a lighthouse to nonbelievers and believers alike.

True-blue Christians do not bow before the idols of material possessions, money, and addictions like alcohol, drugs, food, and sex. Rather, God is number one in their hearts. Followers of Jesus strive to live as he taught—with integrity and love for all, especially the needy, the unloving, and unloved. Catholic home décor may include a crucifix, religious statues and pictures, and palm fronds. We Catholics follow age-old practices such as receiving ashes on Ash Wednesday, observing Good Friday in reverent silence, and gathering for Adoration of the Cross with the community of faith. We pray together as a family and are a force for good in our neighborhoods. Our Bibles are not dusty; the pages are dog-eared from being read and pondered. We actively participate in Mass by praying aloud and singing. We join parish organizations and support parish ministries. We take steps to expand our knowledge about the Church and its teachings. We don't hesitate to speak about the faith and defend it.

Our fervor for our Catholic faith just might prove to be as contagious as was the faith of Chi.

Response

If you were arrested for being a Christian, would there be enough evidence to convict you? Make one change in your home or your life that clearly sends this message: "I am a Catholic."

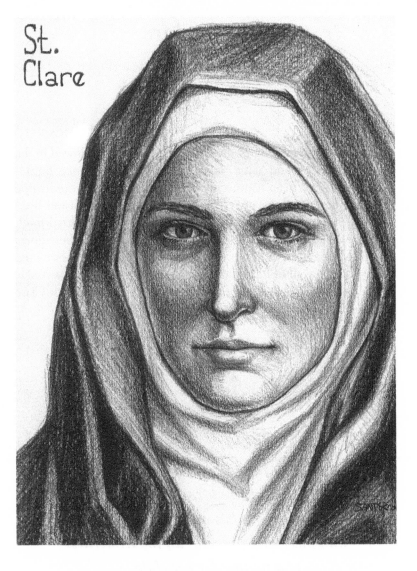

St.
Clare

Go in peace. You have followed the good way.
Go in confidence because your Creator
has sanctified you, has cared for you constantly,
and has loved you with all the tenderness
of a mother for her child....
Blessed be you, my God, for having created me.

Saint Clare

1193–1253 • Virgin, Religious • August 11

LIFE

Born of a wealthy family in Assisi, Italy, Saint Clare followed in the footsteps of her friend Saint Francis and, with his guidance, founded the first Franciscan community for women. Clare wrote its rule and served as abbess for forty-two years. The cloistered Sisters lived a life of prayer, penance, and silence, subsisting on donated food. Today these Sisters are known as the Poor Clares. Once when illness prevented her from going to Mass, Clare miraculously viewed the liturgy on the wall of her room. Consequently, she is the patroness of television. Her remains are housed at the Basilica of Saint Clare in Assisi. She addressed her last words to herself and to God.

LAST WORDS

Go in peace. You have followed the good way.
Go in confidence because your Creator
has sanctified you, has cared for you constantly,
and has loved you with all the tenderness
of a mother for her child....
Blessed be you, my God, for having created me.

Reflection: The Gift of Life

Today visitors to the Poor Clare monastery in Assisi can view the corner of the plain room where Saint Clare died. Above the site, a plaque reads, "Blessed be you, my God, for having created me." What a perfect way to end one's life—praising the God who made it all possible!

We believe God planned our being before time existed. Then he arranged for the right two people to meet, marry, and provide the unique DNA that makes us who we are. Today our Creator sustains us—every breath and every heartbeat are dependent on him. As Saint Augustine said, "God loves us as if there were only one of us."

Because God endowed us with human life, we are capable of marvelous things. We can thrill to music and birdsong, run with wind blowing through our hair, dance, swim, savor food, read, and play a musical instrument. We can know the satisfaction of mastering algebra and French and learning how to cook and build a house. We can create new things: a recipe, a song, a quilt, or piece of art. We can imagine, remember, solve problems, and make decisions.

Because we are alive, the whole cosmos is our playground. We are free to explore the universe and gaze in awe before natural wonders like the Grand Canyon, Niagara Falls, and star-studded night skies. We can be astonished by flora from the lowly fern to the giant redwood, to say nothing of fauna like the exotic peacock, the graceful deer, and our own pet.

Arguably the most precious blessing human life affords is love in all its forms. We know the love of God and the love of parents, spouse, children, family, and friends. We also experience the intoxicating joy of loving others in return.

The original meaning of *thank* is "to think of." It is only right, then, that we pause from time to time to think of and thank God for the tremendous blessing of our life. Jesus explained that he came to earth that we might have life in abundance. As his followers, we are called to work and pray that every person God created may enjoy life to its fullest.

Response

What are five of your favorite things? Thank God for each of them.

Saint Cyprian

?–258 • Bishop, Martyr • September 16

LIFE

Despite the opposition of some Church members, Saint Cyprian served as bishop of Carthage in North Africa for ten years. He was renowned for his writings, eloquent speaking, and holiness. During a plague, he encouraged Christians to help victims, even those who were enemies. Cyprian was no stranger to conflict. He supported Pope Cornelius when he was threatened by a false claimant to the papacy. He dealt with clergy who believed that all apostates, even the unrepentant, should be accepted back into the Church. Finally, for refusing to sacrifice to idols, Cyprian was exiled and then imprisoned. When he heard the method of his execution—beheading by the sword—he spoke his final words.

LAST WORDS

Thanks be to God.

Reflection: Courage to Do What Is Right

In 1648, the Superior General of the Jesuits founded the Bona Mors Confraternity. *Bona mors* is Latin for "happy death." Members were given guidance in living well to facilitate a graceful passing from this world. Judging from his dying words, Saint Cyprian had a very happy death. He hailed the announcement of his beheading with a prayer of gratitude. In fact, in the last moments of his life, he gave the executioner twenty-five gold pieces!

We might conjecture that Cyprian welcomed death as a relief from the sufferings he endured in life. Always taking a stand for what was right, he was embroiled in one conflict after another. Sometimes we find ourselves in situations that require us to summon the courage to act with integrity. We may hold an opinion contrary to one professed by the majority. In that case, we might be swayed to join them or at least refrain from voicing our opinion. We may be in a position to be a whistleblower, while others who know something is wrong take no one action to stop it. By doing the right thing, we risk ruining our reputation, our career, or a friendship. Like Cyprian, we may even be pressured by threats of torture and death to act against our principles. In times like these, the Holy Spirit—our Advocate who dwells within us—is poised to activate the gift of fortitude we first received at Baptism.

Cyprian probably made a habit of accepting his crosses as a share in the sufferings of Christ. Then, instead of viewing his death as an escape, he greeted the news of his imminent death with joy, knowing he would soon see the Lord face-to-face.

Response

When your conscience urges you to stand up for something that's right, take action, even though it may be inconvenient, uncomfortable, or risky. Pray that those who are being tested right now may uphold what is true and good.

Saint David

c. 500–589 • Bishop • March 1

Life

Saint David was a Welsh bishop renowned for his teaching and preaching. He presided over two synods called to confront Pelagianism, a heresy which denies original sin and teaches that human beings can achieve salvation without grace. David founded many monasteries and churches throughout the land, including David's Cathedral, which still stands on the site of one of his monasteries in Wales. His rule for the monks called for strict asceticism. Saint David's Day is an annual Welsh celebration.

Last Words

Be joyful, hold fast to the faith,
and do the little things
that you have seen me do and heard about.
I will walk the path that our fathers
have trod before us.

Reflection: The Importance of Little Things

Once when I was in charge of music for a Mass at our convent retreat house, things went very wrong. I arrived too late to begin the opening song, I started one song too high, and so on. After that fiasco, I sat in the chapel feeling ashamed and miserable. As the other sisters filed out, one of them gave my shoulder a little squeeze. Suddenly things weren't so bad.

To this day Saint David's "Do ye the little things in life" is a popular Welsh expression. His last words are excellent advice. Who doesn't know the importance of a little act of kindness? Small things can transform a gloomy day into a sunny day full of promise. Mark Twain once claimed, "I can live for two months on a good compliment." Most of us will not make an impact on the world by monumental, colorful, and impressive actions. We will not appear on the evening news or the cover of *Time Magazine*. We can, however, achieve greatness, not to mention holiness, by performing small deeds well. As Saint Teresa of Calcutta noted, "Not all of us can do great things. But we can do small things with great love."

What are some small, seemingly insignificant deeds that can make a significant difference? Calling an old friend just to say hi, sending a sympathy card, emailing a word of encouragement, giving your place in the checkout line to someone with only a few items, and smiling at someone are examples of acts that infuse joy, hope, and peace in the hearts of friends, family, and strangers. Jesus himself taught the value of little things. He said, "Whoever is faithful in a very little is faithful also in much" (Luke 16:10).

Vincent van Gogh said, "Great things are done by a series of small things brought together." One great thing achieved by doing many small things is a sign of a beautiful, meaningful life that culminates in eternal life.

Response

What little things did people do for you this week that made a difference in your life? Do a little thing today that will make a difference for someone else.

Saint Dismas

?–c. 30 • Layman • March 25

Life

Saint Dismas is one of the names traditionally assigned to the "good thief" crucified with Jesus. He might have been a rebel against Roman rule or a cold-blooded murderer. According to the Gospel of Luke, Dismas rebuked the other man being crucified with them when the man mocked Jesus. He pointed out that they were getting their just deserts, while Jesus was innocent. When Dismas asked Jesus to admit him into his kingdom, Jesus promised that he would enter Paradise that very day. In a way then, Dismas stole his way into heaven.

Last Words

Jesus, remember me
when you come into your kingdom.

Reflection: Salvation at the Last Minute

Actor John Wayne, who called himself the "cardiac Catholic," snuck into heaven under the wire, converting to Catholicism on his death-bed after a less-than-virtuous life. He had been married three times and had several affairs, but his profession of faith superceded every indiscretion.

God's saving grace is a mystery. This is true in the case of Saint Dismas. After chiding the other criminal for mocking Jesus, he made an act of faith, acknowledging that Jesus is a king. Grace prompted Dismas to perform this final good act that absolved him of the sins of his entire life. His is the only instance in Scripture of the guarantee of heaven. (Of course, the Church, guided by the Holy Spirit, assures us that Mary and the saints are citizens of heaven too.)

One of Jesus' parables makes us think of the saving of Dismas: the parable of the employer who pays equal wages to all workers regardless of hours worked. (See Matthew 20:1-16.) This story disturbs us. It goes against our sense of fairness. We sympathize with the outraged workers who toiled longer in the vineyard, but we understand the generosity and mercy of the employer for the men who worked only an hour. Similarly, last-minute conversions show the boundless mercy of God. He is ever the good shepherd seeking the wandering sheep in danger. He is the loving Father welcoming home a wayward child. He is the father who throws a lavish party when his prodigal son returns. Are we ever like the resentful righteous brother? Would we join the celebration? Are we as prodigal with mercy as God is with those who profess him at the end of their lives?

As God's children, how can we refuse to rejoice when he acts with incredible, incomprehensible love? Over the course of our lifetime God forgives us more times than we can count. Nothing can disqualify us in the race to the Father. In a way, we all are thieves of heaven.

Response

Some sinners have no one to pray for them. Say a prayer for those who are dying today most in need of mercy and the assurance of God's love.

Saint Dominic

1170–1221 • Priest, Religious, Founder • August 8

LIFE

Saint Dominic, born in Spain, was highly educated. He became a priest and an outstanding preacher. To combat the rampant Albigensian heresy, he founded a convent for the religious education of children. He also spread the Gospel by preaching and by giving good example. He was the founder of the Order of Preachers, also known as Dominicans, the men who joined him in carrying out this work. Their poverty and austerity persuaded people they met in Italy, Spain, and France to accept their teachings as true. Dominicans also promoted praying the rosary. In his last words, Dominic prayed to God and spoke a single word to his friars: "Begin." Then he repeated the prayer being offered by those around his deathbed.

LAST WORDS

Holy Father, as you know I have persevered with all my heart in following your will. And I have carefully kept those whom you have given me. I commend them to you. Preserve them and keep them.

Begin.

Come to his assistance, you saints of God, meet him, you angels of the Lord, receiving his soul, offering it in the sight of the Most High….

REFLECTION: ANGELS

In 2013, a car accident left nineteen-year-old Katie Lenz pinned between the steering wheel and the seat. As the rescue crew tried unsuccessfully to free her, Katie asked if someone would pray aloud. A priest appeared, prayed with her, anointed her, and disappeared. Katie was freed and flown to the hospital by a flight for life. No one could identify the priest, and he didn't appear in photographs of the scene. News reports left people wondering: Was this an angel? After a few days the "angel" came to light in the form of Father Patrick Dowling.

People jumped to the conclusion that an angel comforted the girl because that is what angels do. These magnificent creatures are pure spirits like God, but created, and possess powers far surpassing ours. Their main function is to endlessly give glory to God in heaven. Some angels, however, are charged with guarding and guiding human beings. It is believed that one of their tasks is to usher us from this world into the next. The prayer offered at Saint Dominic's deathbed, the *Subvenite*, refers to these angelic escorts. Today this prayer is said or sung at the conclusion of a funeral liturgy.

Although some people scoff at the idea of angels and devils, we have ample evidence of their existence. Scripture from Genesis to Revelation is filled with angels, and the Catholic Church asserts that angels are personal, immortal beings created by God. Some saints like Padre Pio and Gemma Galgani conversed with their guardian angels. In addition, stories about angelic rescues abound. In these skeptical times, surveys reveal that most people believe in angels.

As we participate in the Eucharist, we are joining in the ongoing heavenly liturgy, a prelude to the time when human beings will join the angels in praise God for all eternity. Saint John Bosco once advised, "Ask your angel to console and assist you in your last moments." No doubt Dominic was accompanied to heaven by his guardian angel.

RESPONSE

Take the advice of Pope Pius XII: "We should get to know the angels now if we wish to spend eternity with them." Be aware of your guardian angel. Thank your invisible friend for companioning you on your earthly journey.

Saint Dominic Savio

1842–1857 • Youth • March 9

LIFE

Saint Dominic was born in Italy, one of ten children. A very religious boy, he was permitted to make his first Holy Communion years before the customary age. When he was twelve, he confided his desire to be a priest to Saint John Bosco. While in Don Bosco's school, he was known for his holiness. A born leader, he organized a club called the Company of the Immaculate Conception in which members gave service to the school. Poor health forced Dominic to leave the school, and he died shortly after his fourteenth birthday.

LAST WORDS

What wonderful things I am seeing!

Reflection: Visions of Heaven

For many children, going to an amusement park is the highpoint of the summer. It is an enchanting place where they are charmed by a rollercoaster, a Ferris wheel, cotton candy, merry music, and other delights. When Saint Dominic was on the threshold of heaven, he glimpsed something much more fascinating than an amusement park. Unfortunately, no one asked the obvious question: "What do you see?" Even though we are left in the dark, we can conjecture what appeared so wonderful.

Perhaps Dominic had his first look at heaven itself, full of brilliant light, vivid colors, and amazing creatures. A throng of the holy men and women who preceded him, including his favorite saints, might have been assembled as far as his eye could see. All shining and beautiful, they would have been singing the praises of their Maker with a host of angels. Maybe friends and family members who had preceded Dominic in death were walking toward him to greet him.

It could be that Dominic beheld the Lord Jesus himself in all his dazzling glory, in the same way as he was revealed to the three apostles in the Transfiguration. Jesus might have welcomed the young boy into his kingdom with a wide smile. With his devotion to Mary, Dominic might have seen her, his heavenly mother. Maybe her arms were outstretched to wrap her son in an embrace.

Whatever the tantalizing, secret vision Dominic enjoyed as he slipped away from earth, we can be sure that the same sight awaits all God's faithful children.

Response

Saint John Bosco nurtured holiness in Dominic. Help a young person in the same way he did. Your parish might offer several opportunities to teach or otherwise mentor young people.

St.
Elizabeth
Ann
Seton

Be children of the Church.
Be children of the Church.

Saint Elizabeth Ann Seton

1774–1821 • Widow, Founder • January 4

LIFE

Saint Elizabeth Ann was born into a wealthy Episcopalian family in New York. She and her husband, William Seton, had five children. When William fell into bankruptcy and became ill, Elizabeth accompanied him to Italy in hopes of a cure. When he died, Elizabeth Ann stayed with a Catholic family and, drawn by the Blessed Sacrament in their chapel, became Catholic. Back in the United States, she was shunned by family and friends because of her conversion. She moved to Maryland, where she opened the country's first Catholic school and founded the Daughters of Charity, the first American religious community. Elizabeth Ann was the first person born in the United States to be declared a saint.

LAST WORDS

Be children of the Church.
Be children of the Church.

Reflection: The Church

Several people are credited with saying, "If you find a perfect church, join it. Then it won't be perfect anymore." Many of us "cradle Catholics," who have belonged to the Church from infancy, tend to take our faith for granted. We don't know what it is like to be without it. Saint Elizabeth Ann, who had to think and pray her way to becoming Catholic, recognized that this membership is a precious gift and privilege. The Catholic Church is not perfect, but it can be traced directly back to Jesus Christ.

In the baptistry of Saint John Lateran, the Pope's cathedral, an inscription reads: "Here a people is born of divine stock, generated by the Holy Spirit that fertilizes these waters; Mother Church gives birth to her children in these waves." The Church joined us to the family of God through the waters of Baptism, waters sometimes compared to the water in the womb. All during our lives, like a good mother, the Church nourishes and safeguards our divine life through the seven sacraments and her guidance. When our time on earth has run out, she offers the Anointing of the Sick with its final opportunity for Reconciliation. She comforts us with the Eucharist as Viaticum, bringing us Jesus as a companion on the journey from this world into the next.

As good children of Mother Church, we love her and stay close to her even when her all-too-human side predominates. We learn about her long history as well as current developments and Church teachings. We make an attempt to live up to the Gospel ideals she puts before us. We take advantage of the sacrament of the Eucharist that binds us more intimately to Jesus and to our brothers and sisters in Christ. When someone attacks the Church, we are quick to defend her. We are eager to build the Church by attracting new members to share in the supernatural life she offers and by praying for the Church, who never ceases to pray for us.

Response

Be on the offensive in the new evangelization effort. Invite a family member or friend who has left the Church to go with you to a parish function. Join the evangelization committee in your parish—or begin one!

Saint Elizabeth of Hungary

1207–1230 • Widow, Third Order Franciscan • November 17

LIFE

Saint Elizabeth, daughter of the King of Hungary, was married to Louis IV, a German duke, at age fourteen. Her husband supported her life of prayer, sacrifice, and service, but his mother and other members of court mocked her. When Louis died after six years of marriage, Elizabeth's in-laws forced her and her three children out of the palace. Her uncle, a bishop, sheltered them until her husband's friends could restore them to their home. Elizabeth became a member of the Third Order of Saint Francis and established a hospital where she cared for the poor.

LAST WORDS

O Mary, come to my help! The moment has arrived when God summons his friend to the wedding feast. The Bridegroom seeks his spouse... Silence!... Silence!

Reflection: The Value of Silence

In a musical composition, the rests or silences between the notes can contribute almost as much to its beauty as the notes do. Likewise, the quiet pauses in our lives enhance the beauty of our days. Fabulous things happen in the womb of silence: flowers blossom, snow falls, and poetry is written. Spiritual writer Henri Nouwen called silence and solitude "the furnace in which transformation takes place." Yes, silence *is* golden.

According to Saint John of the Cross, silence is God's first language. Naturally, silence plays an important role in prayer. Surely it's easier to concentrate without the noise of machines, electronic devices, and conversation. In stillness we are more apt to be aware of our invisible but all-present God and we are better attuned to God's soft voice speaking to our hearts. This is the lesson of one of the stories about the prophet Elijah. God had sent Elijah to a mountain to wait for him. While Elijah waited, a rock-blasting wind was followed by an earthquake and then a fire. But God was in none of these deafening events. Only when there was sheer silence, did Elijah hear the voice of God. (See 1 Kings 19:11-13.)

Two people who are deeply in love are content to be silent with each other. For them it is profoundly satisfying just to be near the beloved. Those who yearn for a deeper relationship with God create shrines of silence for themselves. Each day they manage to be alone with the Alone, perhaps by rising early. They might seek out a favorite quiet place to commune with God or wordlessly bask in his presence. Occasionally they participate in a day of recollection or make a weekend or week-long retreat, taking refuge from the clamor of their busy lives. Surely Saint Elizabeth was familiar with the Scripture verse "Be still, and know that I am God!" (Psalm 46:10). It's no wonder that when she was on the brink of encountering God face-to-face, Elizabeth called out, "Silence! Silence!"

Response

Each day allow yourself the luxury of enjoying a few minutes of silence in order to hear God's voice. After all, God gives you the entire twenty-four hours!

Saint Elizabeth of Portugal

1271–1336 • Widow, Third Order Franciscan • July 4

LIFE

Saint Elizabeth was named after her great-aunt, Saint Elizabeth of Hungary. At a young age, she married the king of Portugal and bore two children. She loved the poor and built institutions to care for them. A peacemaker, she once reconciled her husband and son by riding into battle and forcing them to stop fighting. Another time, when her son and his son-in-law, the king of Castile, were at war, she settled their dispute. After her husband died, Saint Elizabeth became a member of the Third Order of Saint Francis and lived with the Poor Clare nuns. Her last words were addressed to Queen Beatrice, who was at her bedside.

LAST WORDS

Draw up a chair for the radiant lady in white who is coming. Mary, Mother of grace.

Reflection: Mary as Mediator

Saint Elizabeth called Mary "the Mother of grace" while waiting for the Blessed Virgin to accompany her home. The Church has long held that Mary is the Mediator of all graces. The Second Vatican Council's *Constitution on the Church* explained that this is true in two senses. First, Mary let grace flood the earth by cooperating in the Savior's work in a singular way. She willingly became his mother and then, watching him die, shared his suffering. Second, Mary channels the gifts of eternal salvation from God to us. As Saint Bernard said, "God wishes us to have everything through Mary's hands." Saint Bernardine of Siena concurred. He taught, "Every grace that is communicated to this world has a threefold course. For by excellent order, it is dispensed from God to Christ, from Christ to the virgin, from the virgin to us." Of course, the *Constituion on the Church* clarifies that the titles of Mary, including Mediator, must be understood in a way that "neither takes away from nor adds anything to the dignity and efficaciousness of Christ the one mediator."

In 1830, Saint Catherine Labouré had a vision of Mary as Mother of grace in which rays coming from rings on her fingers fell on Earth. Mary explained to Catherine that these rays were graces for those who asked for them and asked to have a medal minted with this image of her. The medal became known as the Miraculous Medal. The Jesuit poet Gerard Manley Hopkins presented lovely metaphors in his poem, "The Blessed Virgin Compared to the Air We Breathe," in which he wrote that Mary "mothers each new grace that does now reach our race." The Church celebrates Our Lady, Mother of Divine Grace on July 23.

Response

What is your most troublesome worry or most pressing need? Place it in Mary's hands now with confidence.

Saint Elizabeth of the Trinity

1880–1906 • Religious • November 8

LIFE

Saint Elizabeth was born on a French military base where her father was a captain. She was a bad-tempered seven-year-old when her father died, but from the age of eleven Elizabeth had a growing devotion to the Blessed Trinity. She taught religion, visited the sick, sang in the choir, and was a gifted pianist. To the dismay of her mother and several suitors, Elizabeth entered a Discalced Carmelite monastery. There she developed a spirituality centered on deepening her love for God. She wished to be called "praise of glory" in heaven and desired that everyone would seek union with God. After suffering for months from Addison's disease, Elizabeth died at age twenty-six.

LAST WORDS

I am going to Light, to Love, to Life!

Reflection: The Indwelling of the Trinity

Once when Saint Catherine of Siena was struggling with temptations, she prayed, "Lord, where were you when those temptations assailed me?" Jesus responded, "I was in your heart." At our Baptism the Blessed Trinity takes up residence within us. We become a walking temple of God. Saint John of the Cross affirmed this, saying, "Thou soul, most beautiful of creatures who longs to know where your beloved is, you yourself are that very tabernacle where he dwells." He advocated giving attention, or "loving remembrance," to God living in us.

Right now the Trinity is in the center of our being. The Father is begetting the Son, and in mutual love they are breathing forth the Spirit. Their dynamic life pulsates in us, abides in us. God within us is as real as in the Blessed Sacrament. He is more intimate to us than we are to ourselves. John Henry Cardinal Newman explained that this divine presence is like light pervading a building or a sweet perfume lingering in the fold of some honorable robe.

This indwelling is central to our existence. Our destiny, when we will reach fulfillment, is communion with God. We are made to seek the knowledge and love of God in a personal sharing of the Trinity's life itself. Created to praise God's glory, we long for complete union with him. We yearn to rest in the infinite love that is God. By making our souls their sanctuary, the Trinity already leads us into the mystery of this divine life. Eternal life is today. How often do we think of the marvel of God-in-us? Saint Elizabeth was well aware that God had made a home in her. During her short life she pondered this mystery in silence, sank down into the immensity of God within her, and anticipated the day she would see God face-to-face. She knew that in the next world she would live forever with the One who was her light, love, and life.

Response

Elizabeth is known for her beautiful prayer, "Holy Trinity, Whom I Adore." Locate this prayer on page 217, reflect on it, and pray it.

Saint Frances of Rome

1384–1440 • Widow, Founder • March 9

LIFE

Married at age thirteen, Saint Frances of Rome was a good wife for forty years and the mother of three sons. With her husband's sister-in-law, she nursed patients in a hospital on a daily basis. She donated her goods to the poor and, when it was needed, turned her house into a hospital. Through patient love she overcame her daughter-in-law's antipathy toward her. She founded the Oblates of Saint Mary to serve the poor and joined the order after her husband's death. It's said that for twenty-three years Frances was able to see her guardian angel, who accompanied and protected her as she walked the streets of Rome, ministering to the poor.

LAST WORDS

The angel has finished his task.
He beckons me to follow him.

Reflection: Guardian Angels

As a young girl was about to step off the school bus, she felt herself restrained by an arm although no one was near. Suddenly a car careened past the bus. If the girl had crossed the street as usual, she would have been struck. For the rest of her life, she believed that her guardian angel had saved her. Even as a religious sister in her nineties, she kept a picture of an angel guiding children above her bed.

The Church teaches that God assigns each of us a personal guardian angel. This belief is anchored in words of Jesus: "Take care that you do not despise one of these little ones; for, I tell you, in heaven their angels continually see the face of my Father in heaven" (Matthew 18:10). Guardian angels protect us from evil and are a reassurance in what can be a frightening world. In addition, they give us suggestions for good acts, pray for us, and present our prayers to God. Our invisible friends are a sign of God's love and providential care. That such majestic creatures are charged with leading us safely to heaven underscores our dignity as human beings.

Saint Frances had the rare privilege of knowing her angel, who appeared to her in the form of a boy. He cast light before her as she traversed the Roman streets at night on her errands of mercy. When Frances acted in an unsaintly manner, her angel would fade or disappear. Other saints were keenly aware of guardian angels. Saint Louis de Montfort ended letters with "Greetings to your guardian angel." Saint Pope John XXIII disclosed that he prayed to his guardian angel at least five times a day, and he once credited his guardian angel for inspiring him with the idea of calling for the Second Vatican Council.

Most people seldom give a thought to their powerful bodyguard. Not only would it be good to be mindful of our angels, but we should, as Saint Bernard of Clairvaux recommended, express our gratitude to them for the great love with which they obey God and help us.

Response

Some people invoke their guardian angel's protection in "traveling prayers." Pray to your guardian angel before you drive or undertake anything else where your life is at risk.

Saint Francis of Assisi

c. 1181–1226 • Religious, Founder • October 4

Life

In the crumbling San Damiano Church in Assisi, Saint Francis, the son of a wealthy merchant, heard a voice command, "Repair my house, which is falling into ruin." Francis responded by selling his father's cloth in order to donate to the church. Brought before the bishop by his father for stealing, Francis gave away everything, donned a brown robe tied with rope, went barefoot, and became a beggar. Once Francis realized that he was called to renew not just the church of San Damiano, but the whole Church, the people of God, he began to preach. Others joined him and became the Friars Minor, the Poor Clares, and the Third Order of Franciscans. Francis rejoiced in creation and was the first to make a life-size Nativity scene, using live animals. During a vision he received the stigmata, Christ's wounds. His last words were spoken after he asked his friars to lay him on the ground. After those words, he sang Psalm 142.

Last Words

I have done what was mine to do;
may Christ teach you what you are to do.

REFLECTION: PSALMS

The eighth-grade lector at a school Mass was unfamiliar with the word *fidelity*. He proclaimed, "The psalm response is 'the fiddle-dee-dee of the Lord remains forever.'" The student body faithfully repeated this response and continued to do so after each verse.

The psalms we pray at Mass and in the Liturgy of the Hours are from the Old Testament Book of Psalms. This was the prayer book of the Jewish people, including Jesus and Mary, who probably knew them by heart. Psalms are song-prayers originally prayed in the Temple or on the way to it. Many of our contemporary hymns are psalm verses set to music. Saint Francis liked to sing. Sometimes he would pick up a stick in the woods, pretend to play a violin with it, and sing French songs his mother had taught him. It's no surprise that Francis, whose whole life was a hymn to God, left earth praising God with a psalm.

Although the Jewish word for *psalm* means praise, psalms convey a variety of human emotions. Some glorify God with exuberance, and others thank God or ask for mercy and forgiveness. The majority of psalms are laments, complaints in which the psalmist looks to God for help. For example, Psalm 142, Saint Francis' swan song, is appropriate for times of distress. Its last verse begins, "Bring me out of prison, so that I may give thanks to your name." In Psalm 22 and other messianic psalms, Christians discern a prophecy of Christ.

Because psalms are poetry, they are packed with figurative language. For example, God is shepherd, fortress, and rock. He tenderly collects our tears in a bottle. Enemies are like buzzing bees, while the psalmist compares himself to a lonely bird on a rooftop.

Down through the ages, people have treasured the psalms. Saint Augustine said, "My psalter is my joy." Dorothy Day, co-founder of the Catholic Worker Movement, declared, "My strength returns to me with my morning cup of coffee and reading the psalms." They have been called the runway to God, which is precisely how Francis used Psalm 142—a runway to God and eternal life.

RESPONSE

What is your favorite psalm? Why? Memorize it. Then find another psalm that expresses what is in your heart.

Saint Francis de Sales

1567–1622 • Bishop, Doctor of the Church, Founder • January 24

LIFE

Saint Francis was born to a noble family in Savoy, France. From an early age, he had a desire to be a priest. However, to please his father, he obtained doctorates in law and theology, and learned the gentlemen's pursuits of riding, dancing, and fencing. Then instead of marrying the heiress his father chose for him, he signed over his inheritance to his younger brother and was ordained a priest. In addition to being a renowned preacher, he wrote and distributed weekly essays explaining the faith. Francis became bishop of Geneva, Switzerland, and with Saint Jane Frances de Chantal founded the Order of the Visitation. He was outstanding in guiding people in the ways of holiness. His book *The Introduction to the Devout Life* is still read today.

LAST WORD

Jesus.

Reflection: The Power of Jesus' Name

The name *Jesus* was as common among Jewish people as the surname *Smith* is among Americans. However, in Hebrew, it was *Yeshua, Joshua,* or *Isaiah.* Our English word *Jesus* is derived from the Greek translation. No matter what form this holy name takes, it is dynamic, standing for our all-holy Lord and Savior. In the Church's infancy, Peter worked a healing miracle in the name of Jesus. A crippled man sprang up, walked, and leaped for joy. (See Acts 3:1-10.) It is said that devils tremble at hearing the awesome name of Jesus.

The name of Jesus is efficacious. It is not a magic charm. The person pronouncing the name must have an intimate friendship with our Lord. Jesus promised that whatever we ask of the Father in his name, we will obtain. That is why liturgical prayers end with "We ask this in the name of our Lord Jesus Christ." The Son of God is our mediator, our spokesperson, whom the Father never fails to hear and heed. When we invoke the name of Jesus, we invoke his power and authority. Not only are we to petition in Jesus' name, but we are also to give "thanks to God the Father at all times and for everything in the name of our Lord Jesus Christ" (Ephesians 5:20).

Saint Peter declared, "Everyone who calls on the name of the Lord shall be saved" (Acts 2:21). Saint Francis de Sales is one of the many saints whose dying word was the name of Jesus. This saint poured himself out teaching others the way to salvation. How right that he wrapped up his life by pronouncing the name that in Hebrew means "God is salvation."

Response

When have you called on the name of Jesus? As an act of reverence and love, adopt the habit of bowing your head whenever you hear this holy name.

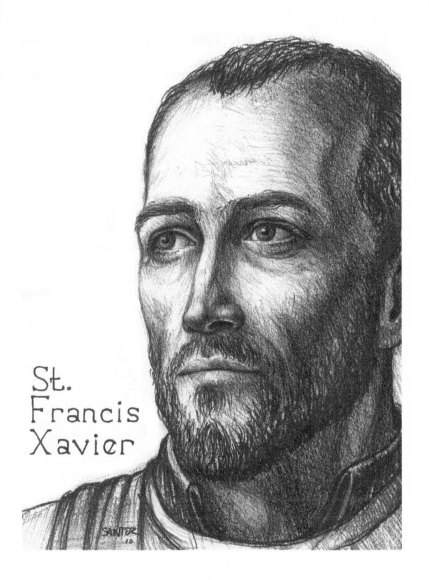

St.
Francis
Xavier

Jesus.

Saint Francis Xavier

1506–1552 • Priest, Religious • December 3

Life

Born in Spain of a noble family, Saint Francis was studying at the University of Paris when he met Saint Ignatius, a fellow student. One day, echoing Jesus, Ignatius asked Francis, "What does it profit a man if he gains the whole world but loses his soul?" This prompted Francis to channel his leadership qualities and ambition into teaching people about God. He and five others joined Ignatius to form the Company of Jesus (Jesuits). After his ordination, Francis became a missionary in India, Malaysia, and Japan. While on the voyage to fulfill his dream of ministering in China, he became ill and died on an island within sight of his goal.

Last Word

Jesus.

REFLECTION: THE HOLY NAME OF JESUS

In the fifteenth century Saint Bernardine preached throughout Italy, promoting devotion to the Holy Name of Jesus. He carried with him a wooden tablet that bore a painted monogram of the Holy Name (IHS) encircled by sun rays. This monogram was created from the Greek word for Jesus. Bernardine used the tablet in blessing the sick and working miracles. Through his efforts, the word *Jesus* was added to the Hail Mary. The Jesuit logo is composed of Bernardine's emblem with the addition of a cross and three nails.

We can only imagine the challenges and disappointments Saint Francis Xavier endured in the Far East. One hardship he keenly felt was the loneliness of separation from his fellow Jesuits. To ease this loneliness, he used to cut their signatures from their letters and pin them inside his clothes. Focusing on Jesus and praying to him brought him comfort and the stamina to persevere. Jesus was his all. If Francis lived today, he might have a tattoo of the Holy Name. It was Jesus the Lord he was serving. He preached and acted in the name of Jesus. He spent himself introducing others to Jesus. Why? Because he loved Jesus more than all the attractions the world had to offer.

Francis was a faithful Jesuit, a "companion of Jesus." What better way then for such a Christ-centered life to end than by uttering the name of Jesus? Francis Xavier had not gained the world, but he had saved his soul…and the souls of countless others.

RESPONSE

Pray the Litany of the Holy Name of Jesus on page 218. Offer it for the intention of missionaries.

Saint Frederick

c. 780–838 • Bishop, Martyr • July 18

LIFE

Saint Frederick was known for his holiness and knowledge. As bishop of Utrecht in the Netherlands, he faced severe opposition, including the wrath of the Empress Judith when he pointed out her immoral conduct. He also preached to enemies of Christianity in and around his diocese. Consequently, one day after Mass Frederick was stabbed to death by two assassins.

LAST WORDS

I will praise the Lord in the land of the living.

Reflection: The Afterlife

A small boy whose cat had died was sobbing. To comfort him, his dad explained that the cat was in heaven. The boy replied, "What would God want with a dead cat?" This boy's concept of heaven is more in line with the ancient Hebrews' view of *Sheol* than with the Christian heaven. *Sheol* was the land of the dead where people drifted like shadows. On the other hand, the followers of Jesus believe in heaven as the land of everlasting life.

Our hopes are pinned on Jesus Christ. He was not merely resuscitated, as were some biblical characters, but endowed with a glorious new kind of life. Because Jesus rose, we can take his word that we too will someday leave our tombs or graves empty. This was what Saint Frederick held to be true. For him, death signaled his entrance into a new, peaceful life in which he would be free from conflicts. In heaven's realm love prevails.

Living in heaven really doesn't mean resting for all eternity. Rather, heaven's inhabitants have the full-time occupation of carrying out the work for which they were created, namely, praising God. On beholding the splendor of our all-good God face-to-face, the saints and angels glorify Father, Son, and Holy Spirit with all their being. Flooded with peace and sheer bliss, and in the company of all the other holy ones, they are perfectly fulfilled. All day long (there is no night) their voices raised in praise resound for all eternity. But since they are still interested in earth dwellers and bound to us in the Communion of Saints, now and then they come to our aid. Saint Frederick, pray for us!

Response

God is everywhere, but we are not always aware of God's presence. Recall that you are currently in the presence of the Trinity and pray a Glory Be.

Saint Gabriel Possenti

1838–1862 • Religious • February 27

Saint Gabriel was born in Assisi and christened Francis. As a lad, he enjoyed social life and was known as "the dancer." When he fell ill, he promised that if he recovered, he would become a member of a religious community. Once healed, he forgot his promise until he witnessed a procession featuring the image of the Blessed Virgin. Here he heard an inner voice ask why he hadn't entered religious life. Against the wishes of his family, Francis joined the Passionists and received the name Gabriel of Our Lady of Sorrows. Before ordination, however, he contracted tuberculosis. At the moment of death, he sat up, his face radiant, and reached out his hand.

Last Words

Jesus, Mary, Joseph, I offer you my heart and soul.
Jesus, Mary, Joseph, assist me in my last agony.
Jesus, Mary, Joseph, may I breathe forth
my soul with you in peace.

REFLECTION: THE HOLY FAMILY

In the lower crypt of the Basilica of the Immaculate Conception in Washington, D.C., a poignant statue depicts the Holy Family on their journey to Egypt to escape the wrath of King Herod. All three, as well as their donkey, are fast asleep. As human beings, the holy trio needed sleep and eventually, like the rest of the human family, they would end their lives in the sleep of death. Each of these holy persons has a special connection to our death.

The death of Jesus, the innocent God-man, was the most tragic and yet most beneficial in history. By undergoing crucifixion, one of the cruelest means of execution ever contrived, Jesus succeeded in rescuing the human race from eternal death, from damnation. He is our bridge to heaven. The death of Mary is matter for speculation. We believe that God made an exception and gave her the honor and privilege of being admitted into heaven body and soul. Some theologians theorize that Mary, as the all-pure Mother of God, was spared death. Others contend that because Mary's son experienced death, she did too. In the Hail Mary, we ask Mary to pray for us at the hour of our death. Presumably when Saint Joseph breathed his last, both Jesus and Mary were at his side. For this reason we invoke the legal father of Jesus as the patron of a happy death.

As the eleventh of thirteen children, Saint Gabriel knew the strong bonds and comfort of family. When he was dying, he summoned the Holy Family for assistance, praying a common deathbed prayer. He, like others, looked to Jesus, Mary, and Joseph to ease his passage from this world into the next.

RESPONSE

Act to make your family, the domestic church, grow in holiness. Together you might pray, read, and discuss a Scripture passage, carry out an act of mercy, or celebrate the sacrament of Reconciliation.

Saint Gemma Galgani

1878–1903 • Virgin, Mystic • April 11

LIFE

Born in Italy and orphaned at seventeen, Saint Gemma raised her siblings. She was devoted to the poor and to prayer, during which she experienced visions and spoke with Jesus, Mary, her angel, and saints. A beautiful woman, Gemma rejected two marriage proposals. After being sick with meningitis for a year, she was cured through the prayers of Saint Gabriel Possenti. Her ill health and visions, which were suspect, prevented her from joining the Passionist Sisters. At age twenty-one, Gemma received the stigmata, Christ's wounds. After suffering from tuberculosis for five years, she died on Holy Saturday.

LAST WORDS

Now it is indeed true
that nothing more remains to me, Jesus.
I commend to you this poor soul of mine…Jesus.

Reflection: Trust in God's Mercy

Prior to the Second Vatican Council, the Sequence at a funeral Mass was the bone-chilling *"Dies Irae"* ("Day of Wrath"). This hymn described a dreadful judgment day when even "the just ones need mercy." Saint Gemma acknowledged this by referring to herself as "this poor soul."

We might wonder why a saint like Gemma, who lived an exemplary life and who was favored by all kinds of supernatural privileges, referred to herself as "this poor soul." Gemma, who wasn't perfect, probably found things to regret as she reviewed her life. Compared to God, the all-holy One, she was indeed a poor soul.

When Gemma's work on earth was finished and her life drew to a close, she entrusted herself to Jesus, surrendering herself into his safe hands, wounded hands. Jesus fits the definition of a friend, someone who knows all about us and loves us anyway. He values us so highly that he freely became one of us, and suffered torture and death. Jesus restored our opportunity to live forever in perfect bliss. Gemma knew there was no need to tremble before such a loving God.

The Church assures us that Gemma, who conversed with Jesus during her stay on earth, is now enjoying his uninterrupted companionship in heaven. She is truly one of God's "gems."

Response

Become a more prayerful person, aware of God in the world and in you. Renew yourself in praying morning and evening prayers and frequent short prayers during the day.

Saint Gertrude the Great

1256–1302 • Religious, Mystic • November 16

Life

Saint Gertrude, the only woman saint named "Great" so far, was born in Germany. As a child, she was taken to a Benedictine monastery and placed under the care of Saint Mechtilde, who became her good friend. Gertrude received a fine education and joined the religious community. When Gertrude was twenty-five years old, she began having visions that whetted her appetite for theology and deepened her prayer life. She wrote many works on spirituality in Latin. Besides being one of the first to be devoted to the Sacred Heart of Jesus, she promoted praying for the poor souls.

Last Words

When will you come?
My soul thirsts for you, O loving Father.

Reflection: Our Longing for God

When we pray Psalm 42, we state that we long for God as a deer longs for flowing streams. In Psalm 63 we pray that we thirst for God as though we're in a dry and weary land where there is no water. Thirst is a craving signaled by the brain to let us know when our bodies need more water to function well and ultimately to stay alive. It is an ideal metaphor for our longing for God.

We need God in order to be complete, fulfilled, and fully alive. We tumble into this world crying and with an insatiable yearning for our Maker—a God-ache. The French mathematician Blaise Pascal poetically stated that there is a God-shaped hole in every person's heart that cannot be filled by any created thing, but by God alone. Nothing or no one else satisfies us. Saint Augustine described our longing as a restless heart. God made us for himself, and only when we are united with God for eternity will our desire for something more be dispelled. Incredibly, God longs for us more than we long for him.

While on earth Saint Gertrude had an inkling of what it would be like to behold our loving God. This stirred in her a burning desire to remain with him forever. She actually looked forward to death.

When we reach our final destination and stand in the presence of God, our Creator-Father, it will be like coming home. We will feel safe, encompassed and inundated by love, and as refreshed as after drinking an ice-cold glass of water on a blisteringly hot day.

Response

Pray Psalm 42 or Psalm 63. Then sit quietly with your desire for the God who made and loves you.

Pope Saint Gregory VII

1020–1085 • Pope • May 25

Life

Pope Saint Gregory VII was born in Italy and studied in Rome. He became advisor and legate for six popes before becoming pope himself. As the "Reform Pope" he fought against simony, the buying and selling of sacred things, but his chief battle was against lay investiture, the practice of secular rulers appointing Church leaders. With the help of Italian rulers, Gregory persuaded Henry IV, the Holy Roman Emperor, to ask forgiveness for this wrong, but Henry had second thoughts. Gregory excommunicated Henry twice. In the end Pope Gregory was forced into exile at Salerno, Italy, where he remained until his death.

Last Words

I have loved justice and hated iniquity,
therefore I die in exile.

Reflection: Speaking Up for Justice

Batman, Superman, Spiderman, Wonder Woman—all are popular fictional superheroes who combat evil. Pope Saint Gregory VII was a flesh-and-blood hero who took a stand for what was right, even if it meant opposing an emperor. Great courage is required to speak up for truth and justice, especially when you are in the minority or when your opinion is not shared by an authority figure. It is more comfortable, less stressful, and sometimes less dangerous to turn a blind eye and deaf ear to wrongs.

Jesus boldly and repeatedly pointed out the errors of religious leaders. Of course, this led to his execution. His cousin Saint John the Baptist, who dared to rebuke King Herod, met with the same fate. Today we too are challenged to stand up for what is right and to fight for justice. We do this by taking part in protests, writing letters and making phone calls to government officials, circulating petitions, voting, and engaging with others through social media. We may also have the opportunity to speak out at meetings and other gatherings, giving voice to the demands of the Gospel. Doing so might make us lepers, unpopular and even shunned, but chances are we won't be exiled or executed.

Perhaps even more difficult and delicate is the task of confronting people we know—our friends and relatives—when we see they are on a sinful course. Love will empower us to help them see the danger they are in. By our Baptism we share in the prophetic ministry of Jesus. Sometimes we are called to engage in that ministry, bringing people back to our loving and forgiving God.

According to Martin Luther King, Jr., when a person has "some great opportunity to stand up for that which is right and that which is just, and he refuses to stand up because he wants to live a little longer….he may go on and live until he's eighty, and the cessation of breathing in his life is merely the belated announcement of an earlier death of the spirit." Pope Saint Gregory was fully alive, body and soul, in this world until he drew his last breath.

Response

What current issue calls for a prophetic voice? Pray to the Holy Spirit for courage. Then speak up for justice and what is right.

Saint Hugh of Grenoble

1052–1132 • Abbot, Bishop • April 1

LIFE

Saint Hugh, born in France, became a priest and was made bishop of Grenoble at a time when the Church was beset with problems. Longing for a quiet, prayerful life, he resigned as bishop after two years and entered an austere Benedictine order. But because of his success in reforming the Church, Pope Gregory VII ordered him back to Grenoble as bishop. During his fifty-two years serving as a bishop, Hugh used his gift for preaching to defend the Church and bring about improvements in the town of Grenoble. He was also instrumental in founding the Carthusians for giving Saint Bruno the land of Chartreuse for his monastery. His last words were repeated three hundred times during the night of his death.

LAST WORDS

Our Father, who are in heaven, hallowed be your name, your kingdom come, your will be done on earth as it is in heaven. Give us this day our daily bread, and forgive us our trespasses as we forgive those who trespass against us. And lead us not into temptation but deliver us from evil. Amen.

REFLECTION: THE OUR FATHER

Just as the first words we learn are *mama* and *daddy*, so is the Our Father one of the first prayers we learn as members of God's family. In the Rite of Christian Initiation of Adults, the Our Father is presented to the elect as a special inheritance during the last liturgy before they are received into the Church. This fifty-six word prayer is precious because it is from the lips of Jesus in response to the apostles' request to teach them how to pray.

At Mass the priest introduces the Our Father by declaring, "We dare to say." Yes, we dare to call the omnipotent, unnamable, transcendent, utterly-other God our *Father*. God does not want us to regard him as an absentee landlord, an icy force, or a supreme being who lords it over us. Rather, God invites us to address him tenderly as Father. And so we boldly do so. In God's eyes we are more than servants, more than friends; we are his children. Praying, "*Our Father*" reminds us of our union with God's Son Jesus and with all of our brothers and sisters in Christ. The prayer is composed of three petitions centered on God, followed by four petitions that express our needs. These petitions number seven, the perfect number in Jewish tradition.

The third-century theologian Tertullian pointed out that the Our Father is a summary of the whole Gospel. Pope Saint John XXIII stated, "To know how to say the Our Father and to know how to put it into practice, this is the perfection of the Christian life." The *Didache*, an early Church document, recommended praying the Our Father three times a day. The Our Father, in which we plead for our daily bread and forgiveness, also makes an ideal prayer before meals.

Because the Our Father is so familiar, it is easy to glide over it as mindlessly as we recite the alphabet. To focus our attention on its weighty words, we might take Saint Teresa of Avila's advice and spend a whole hour praying it once, pausing after each line to reflect on and savor it. It's obvious that Saint Hugh treasured this essential and intimate prayer.

RESPONSE

Read the detailed explanation of the Our Father in part four, section two of *The Catechism of the Catholic Church*. Look for a copy in your parish library or read it online.

St. Ignatius of Loyola

Oh, God.

Saint Ignatius of Loyola

1491–1556 • Priest, Religious, Founder • July 31

Life

The youngest son of a noble family, Saint Ignatius served as a soldier until he sustained an injury to his legs from a cannonball. During his recovery, he read the life of Christ and the lives of the saints. After a period of prayer, he began to lead an ascetic life and to write his Spiritual Exercises. Following a pilgrimage to Jerusalem, he studied theology and Latin at a university in Spain, where he was much older than his classmates. In 1534 he attended the University of Paris. There he was joined by six men in forming a religious community, known today as the Society of Jesus or Jesuits. They took vows of poverty, chastity, and obedience, but, having offered their service to the pope, took a fourth vow of obedience to the pope. Always in poor health, Saint Ignatius died unexpectedly of a fever in Rome. He did not receive the papal blessing he had requested or the last sacraments. He could be heard repeatedly murmuring his last words throughout the night before he died.

Last Words

Oh, God.

Reflection: Giving God Glory

The Jesuit motto, *Ad majorem Dei gloriam* (For the greater glory of God), reflects the heart of Ignatian spirituality. It proclaims that all actions are performed with the intention of giving glory to God. At one time Catholic school children had the custom of writing the initials *AMDG* on the top of their papers to signify that their schoolwork was done to honor God—and as a reminder to do their best!

Saint Ignatius was driven to live this motto to the nth degree. He believed that God created us, pervades and sustains our world, and is our destiny. This former soldier was captivated by the knowledge that the whole point of our existence is to know God, respond to him with love, and serve him as wholeheartedly as any good soldier would serve his king. Therefore, Ignatius committed himself to the King of the Universe—Father, Son, and Holy Spirit—and, like a general, he led others to do the same. His goal was no longer to win wars but to win people over to Christ, a goal we share today.

The first Jesuits called themselves the Company of Jesus. They dedicated themselves to carrying on the mission of Jesus, spreading the Good News by teaching and missionary work. How fitting that in his last hours, Ignatius was heard to simply say, "Oh, God" over and over. Was this invocation a response to a vision or a plea for help in his death agony? It doesn't matter. Ignatius was focused on the One he had served so well. He is the consummate example of Saint Augustine's dictum, "A Christian should be an alleluia from head to foot."

Response

Our days are a mix of important work and mundane tasks. This week make it a practice before any undertaking to deliberately do it for God's greater glory.

St. Jeanne Jugan

O Mary, my dear Mother, come to me.
You know I love you and how I long to see you.

Saint Jeanne Jugan

1792–1879 • Religious, Founder • August 30

LIFE

Saint Jeanne grew up in France during the French Revolution. Rejecting marriage proposals, she devoted herself to serving the poor, nursing, and working as a servant. One day in 1839 she took into her house an elderly woman who was blind and infirm, even giving up her bed for the woman. This act of charity blossomed into the founding of the Little Sisters of the Poor to care for the aged poor. In this new religious community, Jeanne took the name of Sister Mary of the Cross and found joy in begging for the elderly poor. The priest who was put in charge of the community usurped her title of *founder* and excluded her from any responsibility in governing the Little Sisters. He confined her to the motherhouse where for the last twenty-seven years of her life Jeanne lived in obscurity. The younger sisters did not know she was their founder and the first Little Sister. Jeanne, who treasured "littleness," humbly accepted her humiliations.

LAST WORDS

O Mary, my dear Mother, come to me.
You know I love you and how I long to see you.

REFLECTION: MARY, OUR MOTHER

A bereaved mother stood at the grave as her baby girl was being buried. When she heard the words, "I will take care of her, and I will take care of you," she believed she was being consoled by the Blessed Mother. We call Mary *mother* because of Jesus' words from the cross, declaring to his mother, "Woman, behold your son," and saying to the beloved disciple, "Here is your mother." If we believe that the beloved disciple, thought to be John, was representing all of us who are beloved of Jesus, we believe Mary is our God-given mother too.

How is Mary our mother? Eve, the female origin of the human race, is known as the mother of the living. Mary is our mother on the spiritual plane. Through her cooperation with God in the incarnation and then on Calvary, we received divine life and were born anew. We are God's adopted children—brothers and sisters of Mary's son Jesus. The woman who gave birth to Jesus physically is now mother to his mystical body, the Church. She serves as a model for us, just as our mothers do. Saint John Eudes said, "What a wondrous book is the heart of Mary! Blessed are those who read with understanding what is written there, for they will learn the science of salvation."

Mary acts with a mother's heart. Some five hundred years ago she appeared in Mexico City to Saint Juan Diego, an Aztec peasant. Mary requested that a church be built where her children could come to pray to her. One day instead of meeting her at the appointed time, Juan Diego went to fetch a priest for his dying uncle. Mary waylaid Juan Diego and gently rebuked, "Do you not know that I am your mother?" His uncle lived. As our mother, Mary loves us deeply. Her dream for us is that we live well, that is, according to her son's teachings. She prays for us and anticipates the day when we will be home together with her and Jesus. No wonder Saint Jeanne loved Mary so much.

RESPONSE

Do you need to jumpstart your love for and devotion to Mary? Begin by praying a rosary, meditating on the Joyful Mysteries.

Saint Joan of Arc

1412–1431 • Laywoman, Martyr • May 30

LIFE

When Saint Joan was a shepherdess, her country, France, was losing a war with England. She began to hear voices and saw visions of Saints Michael, Catherine of Alexandria, and Margaret of Antioch. For about five years, the voices helped her to pray and then assigned her a daunting mission: to save Orleans, see that the Dauphin was crowned king, and drive out the English. When Joan led the French forces, they defeated the English at Orleans, the Dauphin was crowned, and towns were regained. But Joan was betrayed and captured by the English. Tried for heresy, she was condemned and burned at the stake. She was only nineteen years old.

LAST WORDS

Jesus, Jesus, Jesus.

Reflection: The Jesus Prayer

Many parishes in the United States have a Holy Name Society, officially called The Confraternity of the Most Holy Names of God and Jesus. This society has a long history tied to the Dominican Order. Its purpose is to promote reverence for the names of God and Jesus. According to *The Catechism of the Catholic Church*, the name *Jesus* is the only one that contains the presence it signifies. When we pray this holy name, we invoke Jesus and call him within us. The name Jesus is at the heart of every Christian prayer. Out of reverence, Jewish people refrain from saying *Yahweh*, the personal name of God. But, in a way, we Christians pronounce this name of God every time we say *Jesus* because it means "Yahweh saves."

The Jesus Prayer is an expanded version of the one-word prayer "Jesus." It is a mantra, a simple prayer prayed over and over. Inspired by the prayer of the publican in Christ's parable and the cry of the blind Bartimaeus, the Jesus Prayer is "Lord Jesus Christ, Son of God, have mercy on me, a sinner." It is believed to have originated with the desert fathers of the fifth century. Since then people, particularly members of Eastern Christian churches, have used the Jesus Prayer as a way to pray without ceasing.

Chosen by God to accomplish the impossible, Saint Joan knew firsthand the power of the name of Jesus. When she rode into battle, she carried a banner bearing the names Jesus and Mary. As she died, overcome by flames and smoke, she drew strength and solace from repeating the holy name and simultaneously gave witness to her love for Jesus. Joan's short life was directed by and entirely surrendered to him. With the name of Jesus on her lips, she won her last battle.

Response

We are often forced to do nothing. We're put on hold on the phone, we wait for an appointment, or we're stuck in a long checkout line. Put these "do nothing" experiences to good use by praying the Jesus Prayer.

Pope Saint John XXIII

1881–1963• Pope • October 11

LIFE

Pope Saint John XXIII, or good Pope John, was kind, simple, and humble. He was born in Italy as Angelo Guiseppe Roncalli. After his ordination in Rome, he was secretary to the Bishop of Bergamo. During World War I, he served in the army as a stretcher bearer and chaplain. Later he became the Italian president of the Society for the Propagation of the Faith. As Archbishop Roncalli, he was Apostolic Visitor to Bulgaria and then Apostolic Delegate to Turkey and Greece. During World War II, he helped save many Jews. In his advanced age, he was elected pope in 1958, leading the Church for fewer than five years. Pope Saint John surprised the world by calling for the Second Vatican Council, launching the Church into an era of renewal. His last words were whispered twice.

LAST WORDS

Lord, you know that I love you.

Reflection: Love in Action

Visiting a hospital, Pope Saint John XXIII asked a boy what he wanted to be when he grew up. The boy replied, "Either a policeman or a pope." "I would go in for the police if I were you," the Holy Father said. "Anyone can become a pope. Look at me!"

Pope John incarnated the Gospel values and served as pope until he died at age eighty-one, far beyond the normal age of retirement. A few days before his death, he commented, "Every day is a good day to live and also to die. As for me, my suitcase is packed, but I am equally ready to carry on working."

Pope John's last words echo the words of his predecessor Saint Peter, whom Jesus entrusted with the care of the Church despite his threefold denial. Jesus graciously allowed Peter to make restitution by asking him not once, but three times, "Do you love me?" And Peter declared his love three times. But there is a litmus test for true love. Unless it is proven by deeds, love is sterile.

Because God speaks personally to us through Sacred Scripture, we can hear Jesus directing the questions he posed to Peter to us. How do we answer when he asks us, "Do you love me?" We can glibly respond with a resounding, "Of course, I love you," but we prove our love is real and sincere by keeping the commandments written by the finger of God and by loving as God loves. Love for our fellow human beings is essential, for as writer François Mauriac warned, "When your heart no longer burns with love, then others will die of the cold." Inside Pope John's plus-sized body was a large heart that warmed the whole world.

Response

Is your love for God passionate or tepid? How do you know? Assure God that you love him by undertaking a loving action. Write a letter or send a card, take the first step in eliminating a bad habit, donate to a worthy cause, or prepare someone a special meal.

Saint John Baptist de le Salle

1615–1719 • Priest, Religious, Founder • April 7

LIFE

Saint John, born to a wealthy French family, was intelligent and cultured. He became a priest and earned a doctorate in theology. As he was helping a community of sisters establish a school for the poor, he met Adrian Nyel, who was starting a free school for poor boys. John's involvement in Nyel's school led to a life-long commitment. He trained laymen to be good teachers and eventually invited them to live with him, paving the way for the founding of the religious community of the Brothers of the Christian Schools. Despite opposition from Church leaders and other educators, John's schools flourished. He died on Good Friday.

LAST WORDS

In all things I adore the will of God in my regard.

Reflection: Discernment

One day the donkey Saint Teresa of Avila was riding threw her off into the mud. Upset, Saint Teresa challenged God, "Why did you let this happen?" God answered, "That's how I treat my friends." The saucy saint retorted, "That's why you have so few of them."

Judging from Saint John's life, he clearly was a good friend of God. A wealthy gentleman, he could have lived a life of ease. Instead he found himself working with poor boys, some of them delinquent. Although he should have been showered with accolades and gratitude for greatly improving the quality of education, he was bombarded with criticism and conflict. In many ways, his life bore out the truth of the maxim, "No good deed goes unpunished." Finally, when a mountain of work still beckoned, God called John home at age sixty-seven.

John may have wondered about these mystifying ways of God, but he accepted God's will for him. In fact, he adored it. In his heart he was convinced that God was good and wise, and he trusted implicitly in God's unfailing love for him.

Many aspects of our lives—our birth family, our talents, other circumstances—are as uncontrollable and unpredictable as the weather. Whenever possible, we can, however, determine some matters for ourselves. We can also use the process of discernment, a word that comes from the Greek word for "sorting out." Discernment involves consulting people who know us, realistically assessing our personalities and capabilities, and gathering all the facts we can about our options. We also must consider what Scripture advises and what the Church teaches. Of course, it also helps to pray for enlightenment. The most important factor in making a decision is listening to what our heart tells us. A sign that we have made the correct decision is that it leaves us with peace.

Centuries after John died, he is still teaching. He teaches us to regard God's will as the lodestar guiding us along the right paths.

Response

Are you struggling with a decision now or facing one in the near future? Ask the Holy Spirit to help you. Then be sensitive and open to what God might be asking of you.

Saint John Bosco

1815–1888 • Religious, Priest • January 31

LIFE

The son of an Italian farming family, Saint John only began his education when he was twelve. Befriended by an elderly priest, he eventually was ordained and became Don (Father) Bosco. Concerned about teenagers in prison, John focused on helping delinquent and disadvantaged boys, even resorting to juggling and magic tricks to attract them. He provided lodging for his boys, prayed with them, and saw that they learned trades. To continue his work, he founded a religious community, the Salesians, and cofounded a woman's congregation, Daughters of Mary Help of Christians, to minister to poor girls. He also wrote religious pamphlets. His last words were spoken to the Salesians gathered around his bed.

LAST WORDS

Love each other as brothers.
Do good to all, evil to none.
Tell my boys that I wait for them all in Paradise.

Reflection: Kindness

Did you know that the first Friday in October is World Smile Day? Harvey Ball from Massachusetts, who created the smiley face image in 1963, declared it so. Ball died some years ago, but a foundation continues to sponsor World Smile Day, encouraging everyone to do an act of kindness to make someone smile. Saint John Bosco would love this idea.

As a master teacher, Don Bosco proved true the adage "You can catch more flies with honey than with vinegar." His successful approach to educating rambunctious boys was to love them and to treat them with kindness and respect. He practiced "preventative education" and discouraged punishment. His dying words reflect his conviction and his experience that charity conquers all.

It is fairly easy to be kind and gentle to people we love, even though we may snap at them occasionally. More challenging is doing good to those who may repel us. And most difficult is responding to people who mistreat us. Our first impulse might be to follow the "eye-for-an-eye" code and get revenge. We can show these "enemies" the loving kindness Jesus commands by recalling that they are made in the image and likeness of God and are precious to him. We might also consider that they may be carrying heavy burdens that, if known to us, would evoke our pity. And, if all else fails, we can grit our teeth, exercise self-control, and offer a short silent prayer.

Sometimes all it takes to diffuse a volatile situation is a soft voice or a smile. Saint Teresa of Calcutta once noted, "Kind words can be short and easy to speak, but their echoes are truly endless." Because of John's kindness, many souls headed in the wrong direction made a 180° turnabout to heaven.

Response

Perform an act of kindness today, maybe more than one.

Saint John Chrysostom

c. 347–407 • Bishop, Doctor of the Church • September 13

Life

Saint John, born in Antioch, studied rhetoric and theology. Living as a hermit for two years, he practiced asceticism to such a degree that he ruined his health. Finally John was ordained a priest. He was such a tremendous preacher and teacher that he received the sobriquet *Chrysostom*, meaning "golden mouth." After he became archbishop of Constantinople, he might have had *Adversity* as his middle name for the many enemies he made as he courageously worked for reform, exhorting people to live the Gospel, and speaking out against injustice. In fact, he was exiled twice. Besides his eloquence, John is known for his practical explanations of Scripture. He spoke his last words on a forced march, as guards moved the frail, dying archbishop from one place of exile to another.

Last Words

Glory to God for all things!

Reflection: Reasons to Praise God

Angels hailed the astounding birth of Jesus by proclaiming, "Glory to God in the highest." In a vision of heaven, every creature in the universe was singing that to God "be blessing and honor and glory and might for ever and ever!" (Revelation 5:13). To give glory to God is to acknowledge and praise God for his divine attributes— majesty, goodness, mercy, love—and his wonderful works. Glorifying God is the purpose of our existence and, with God's grace, how we will spend our eternity.

Inanimate things and animals give glory to God merely by existing. In the third chapter of the Book of Daniel, three men thrown into a furnace sang, "Bless the Lord, stars of heaven; sing praise to him and highly exalt him forever." In their litany, among other things, they addressed winds, fire and heat, dew and falling snow, mountains and hills, whales, and birds of the air. We human beings are higher on the ladder of creation than other creatures in that we have the Godlike abilities to think and choose. Consequently, we are more capable of glorifying God.

Saint John had the wisdom to realize that we owe God glory for all things from the cosmos to our family pets. So, glory to God for gifts that delight us, for challenges that strengthen us, and for sufferings that make us more empathetic. Above all, we praise God for his ingenuity and love that brought us into being and for his compassion that saved us. The Gloria we sing at Mass is a magnificent hymn in which we, God's holy people, unite in adoring him.

As John died, he most likely reviewed his entire life, its joys and its sorrows, giving glory to God for each and every moment. He even may have glorified God for his death, knowing it would usher him into everlasting joy.

Response

Plan a specific way you will give glory to God, perhaps by praying the Glory Be or by doing your job to the best of your ability.

Saint John of the Cross

c. 1541–1591 • Priest, Religious, Founder, Doctor of the Church • December 14

LIFE

Saint John grew up in poverty in Spain. After entering the Carmelite Order, he studied theology and philosophy. He joined with Saint Teresa of Avila in reforming the Carmelites, leading to a new, stricter order, the Discalced Carmelites. Friars who resented these efforts imprisoned him and treated him brutally for nine months. In his tiny cell John, a mystic, prayed deeply and wrote poetry rooted in his spiritual experiences. After escaping, he became a leader of the southern Carmelites and opened new monasteries. He died of a painful disease. His notable works are *The Spiritual Canticle, Ascent of Mount Carmel,* and *The Dark Night of the Soul.*

LAST WORDS

Into your hands I commend my spirit.

Reflection: The Hands of God

"It is a fearful thing to fall into the hands of the living God" (Hebrews 10:31). Those dire words may be true for unrepentant sinners, but do not apply to Saint John. He loved God passionately and spent his life working and suffering for love of him. As John died, he entrusted himself to God, certain that he would fall into good hands.

We were lovingly created by the hands of God, and, as God discloses in Scripture, he has us inscribed on the palms of his hands, a kind of divine tattoo. (See Isaiah 49:16.) Just as human parents have dreams for their children, God desires only what is beneficial for us. Before Jesus set out on his public ministry, his holy hands were callused by manual labor. The hands of Jesus stretched forth to heal the sick and disabled and to gently bestow the peace of forgiveness on sinners. As a parting gift, Jesus used those divine hands to lift bread and wine that would become his presence with us. Finally his hands were pierced by nails, one excruciating phase of his redemptive sacrifice. After Jesus rose with glorified life, his hands bore the scars of his wounds.

Throughout our lives God gives us a helping hand, guiding us on right paths and shielding us from evil. When our time on earth is up, we will appear before God with the story of our lives as an open book. Then, if we have been faithful lovers like John, God will receive us into his kingdom, his hands wide open in welcome.

Response

Say a prayer for those who will die today. Ask that they have the grace to repent of any sins and be rewarded with eternal life.

Saint John Neumann

1811–1860 • Religious, Bishop • January 5

LIFE

Saint John was trained for the priesthood in his native Bohemia. Due to the glut of priests there, he journeyed to America as a missionary and was ordained in New York. He served German immigrants in mission parishes in several states. Seeking companionship, he joined the Redemptorists and became the order's American superior. Later, as bishop of Philadelphia, he oversaw the opening of almost two hundred Catholic schools and dealt with anti-Catholic persecutions. A short, simple, humble man with an accent, John was unpopular and sometimes mocked. His last words were spoken before setting out for a walk during which he suffered a stroke and died.

LAST WORDS

A man must be ready,
for death comes when and where God wills it.

Reflection: Preparing for Death

Saint John had a premonition of his death. He had lived only forty-eight years, but that was all the time he was allotted to walk this planet. In Greek mythology the Fates were three old women who spun each person's life. Atropos was the Fate who decided when and how someone died and then snipped the thread. We, however, believe that God, who knit us together in our mother's womb, determines the moment and manner of our death. We don't have a clue when our life will end any more than we know when the world will end.

We might die from any number of causes. A car accident, an earthquake, a gunshot, a fatal disease, and a meteor on a collision course with earth are a few possibilities, but only one agent of death is earmarked for us. Because the time of our dying is God's secret, it would be smart to heed John's advice and be ready for it at any time no matter what our age.

Time is running out like sand in an hourglass with our name on it. Here are five practical suggestions for a Christian bucket list. If you are at odds with anyone, reconcile. If you are weighed down by a sin, ask God to forgive you. If you owe someone a thank you, say it. If your house is cluttered and bulging with unused items, give some away. If you haven't expressed your love to a loved one, do so today.

It's said that Saint Ignatius was once asked, "What would you do if you knew you would die today?" The saint replied, "I would keep doing what I'm doing." Hopefully when we die, we will be in the midst of doing good, or at least have as good a track record as John.

Response

What do you need to do before meeting your Maker? Draw up your Christian bucket list and begin work today.

St.
John Paul II

Let me go to the house of my Father.

Pope Saint John Paul II

1920–2005 • Pope • October 22

LIFE

Pope Saint John Paul II, dubbed "the Great," was born Karol Józef Wojtyla in Poland. After becoming a priest in 1946 and receiving a doctorate in theology in Rome, he served in Poland as a parish priest, a professor, and archbishop of Krakow, helping end Communist rule in Europe. In 1978, he was elected the first non-Italian pope since 1523. During his long papacy, he visited 129 countries, authored dozens of documents, improved relations with other faiths, and inaugurated World Youth Day. After barely surviving an assassination attempt, Pope John Paul visited his attacker in prison and forgave him. His last words were spoken in his native tongue.

LAST WORDS

Let me go to the house of my Father.

Reflection: Heaven, Our Home

In the film *Wizard of Oz*, Dorothy is whisked to Oz by a tornado. To get back to her family in Kansas, she must click the heels of her red shoes together and say, "There's no place like home" three times. Pope Saint John Paul II would agree with her. However, he would be thinking, not of his home in Krakow but of his home in heaven.

We envision heaven as a place with white clouds, pearly gates, and streets paved with gold. At the Last Supper, Jesus described heaven using the image of a house, telling his disciples and all of us that he was preparing places for us in his Father's house. (See John 14:2.) Transplanted from our original home by the catastrophe of original sin, we are homesick. Fortunately, like the prodigal father in the parable of the prodigal son, God is waiting on the threshold of heaven to welcome us home with open arms. By dying and rising, Jesus, God's son and our brother, obtained the key to the house.

Caught up in the maelstrom of our busy lives, we seldom give a thought to heaven except when someone dies. Yet, through Saint Paul, God urges, "Set your minds on things that are above, not on things that are on earth" (Colossians 3:2). The more we reflect on heaven and its joys, the more likely it is that we will not lose our way. We will focus on amassing treasures in heaven rather than on earth, and our hearts will then be safely ensconced in heaven. (See Matthew 6:19-21.) Before we know it, we will be home for good, like Pope John Paul II.

Response

Meditate or reflect on heaven every once in a while. For example, when a friend dies, recall that you will meet again; when your body aches, look forward to the future life when you will never feel pain; and when you are sad, anticipate the Father's house where there will be no more tears.

Saint Joseph of Cupertino

1603–1663 • Priest, Religious, Mystic • September 18

LIFE

Saint Joseph, born in poverty in Italy, was an awkward and slow-witted boy. In addition, the religious ecstacy he experienced made him absentminded. At age seventeen he applied to a Franciscan community but was rejected due to his ignorance. The Capuchins, a strict Franciscan order, accepted him as a lay brother, but soon dismissed him when the ecstacies inferred with his work. Eventually Joseph became a Conventual Franciscan friar and then a priest. Because of his gift of levitation, he was investigated by the Inquisition. He was sent to Capuchin houses, where he was isolated from people and closely observed for years. Six years before he died, he was allowed to return to a Conventual community. Joseph was known for his holiness, simplicity, and asceticism.

LAST WORDS

Praised be God! Blessed be God!
May the holy will of God be done!

Reflection: God's Holy Will

When the apostles asked Jesus how to pray, he gave them the words of the Our Father, a blueprint for all prayer for all time. We pray this exquisite prayer during the Eucharist and in the rosary. Each time we pray the Our Father we ask, as did Saint Joseph, "Your will be done."

Looking to the Creator to run the universe is plain common sense. Who knows better what should happen than the wisest, all-knowing, and most loving Being? When life unfolds according to our heavenly Father's plan, the result is peace and joy. But because God has graciously endowed us creatures with a free will, we also possess the power to thwart his will, which only leads to misery in one form or another. Adam and Eve were the first to discover those consequences.

The safest course in life is to make sure that our will is in sync with God's will. This is what Mary, the Mother of God, did. She chose to say yes to God's wishes even though her spontaneous commitment promised a unique and mystifying future. Like mother, like son. Although Jesus was aware that God's will for him entailed suffering and a gruesome death, he opted for God's will over his own.

God does not shout or text directions for each decision we face. Yet the Almighty clearly spelled out his will in the Ten Commandments and in the teachings of Jesus. He has planted signs all along our path. Moreover, our conscience, the voice of God within, enlightens us when it comes to determining the right course of action. We are free to trust God as we make our decisions or to ignore his advice and strike out on our own. Who has more credibility?

Response

Pray to the Holy Spirit, our God-sent Counselor, to know and follow the will of God in large matters and small.

Saint Josephine Bakhita

c. 1869–1947 • Virgin, Religious • February 8

LIFE

Saint Josephine was born to a prestigious family in the Sudan. As a child, she was captured by Arab slave traders and forced to walk barefoot for 600 miles. When she forgot her name, traders called her *Bahkita*, or *lucky*. She was sold repeatedly, sometimes to cruel owners. Josephine ended up in Italy in the care of Canossian Sisters. After being declared a free person, she became Catholic and joined the Canossians. Besides serving as cook, sacristan, and portress, she prepared sisters for the African missions. Josephine impressed others by her sanctity and cheerfulness and was greatly loved. She smiled as she spoke her last words.

LAST WORDS

Yes, I am so happy…Our Lady! Our Lady!

Reflection: Our Lady

For years Garrison Keillor entertained thousands of listeners with stories about his fictional town, Lake Wobegon. He dubbed its Catholic church Our Lady of Perpetual Responsibility. This name was prompted by the myriad titles for Mary as Our Lady. In French Our Lady is *Notre Dame*. In Saint Josephine's Italian language, it is *Madonna*. Artistic representations of Mary, with or without her child Jesus, came to be called Madonnas.

Women of superior social rank have often been addressed as *lady*. The title is derived from a word meaning "kneader of bread." Since Mary, the Mother of God, is Queen of angels and saints, she was given the title of *our Lady*. It's certainly fitting for her, the one who gave birth to the Bread of Life.

Down through the centuries, titles for Mary using "Our Lady" became popular. Some titles were in honor of her qualities and roles (Our Lady of the Immaculate Conception, Our Lady of Sorrows, Our Lady of Good Counsel). Some titles referred to Marian devotions (Our Lady of the Rosary, Our Lady of the Miraculous Medal). Others referred to the places where she appeared (Our Lady of Lourdes, Our Lady of Fatima, Our Lady of La Salette). Recently Mary received a new title: Our Lady, Star of Evangelization.

While studying in Germany, Jorge Bergoglio, now Pope Francis, came across a painting called "Holy Mary, Our Lady, Untier of Knots." After he brought a copy home to Argentina, this presentation of Mary inspired widespread devotion. This image and title remind us that although Mary is noble, she is accessible. We can go to her with our knotty problems, and she will intercede for us. She is our Lady, but she is also our Mother.

After a life with more than its share of tough knots, Josephine was blessed with a happy death and the sight of her heavenly mother. She was truly "Lucky."

Response

Which title of Mary most appeals to you? Why? The Basilica of the National Shrine of the Immaculate Conception in Washington, D.C., houses more than seventy chapels and oratories in honor of Our Lady. Take a virtual tour of the basilica at www.nationalshrine. com or, better still, visit it in person.

Saint Julie Billiart

1751–1816 • Virgin, Religious, Founder • April 8

LIFE

As a child in France, Saint Julie suffered shock-induced paralysis when she witnessed a gunshot narrowly missing her father. During the persecution of the French Revolution, the bedridden Julie taught children the faith and counseled women. One time she fled for her life hidden under hay in a farm wagon. With the aid of her wealthy friend Françoise Blin de Bourdon, Julie founded the Sisters of Notre Dame to care for orphans and educate poor girls. When Julie was fifty-three, a priest asked her to pray a novena to the Sacred Heart with him. His secret intention was that she be cured. Consequently, when he told her to stand and walk, she did. In fact, she walked many miles, making 120 journeys, founding schools and convents and visiting the sisters. As revealed to her in a vision, her institute was marked by the cross. Julie suffered betrayal by her sisters and opposition from the clergy. Still, nothing restrained her from repeating, "God is good." Her last words were the Magnificat, the scriptural prayer of our Blessed Mother. A portion of that prayer is printed here.

LAST WORDS

My soul proclaims the greatness of the Lord; my spirit rejoices in God my Savior, for he has looked with favor on his lowly servant. From this day all generations will call me blessed: the Almighty has done great things for me, and holy is his name....

Reflection: Mary's Magnificat

Every day all over the world the Church prays the Magnificat during Vespers (Evening Prayer). This was an appropriate prayer for Saint Julie, a Sister of Notre Dame (Our Lady), to pray at the evening of her life. Her strong devotion to Mary is reflected in her community's custom that every member has *Mary* or some form of it in her religious name.

The Magnificat is woven with Old Testament verses and themes. In the first four verses, Mary praises God for the marvels he has done for her. As she did at the Annunciation, Mary calls herself God's handmaid. She predicts that from then on everyone would call her blessed and humbly acknowledges that her extraordinary life is God's doing.

According to theologian Dietrich Bonhoeffer, the remaining verses make the Magnificat the most revolutionary Advent song. Here Mary describes God's kingdom of justice and peace as a kingdom of reversals, where the proud and mighty are cast down and the lowly are raised up, where the rich are sent away empty while the hungry are filled with good things. When her son Jesus proclaims his mission, he ascribes the words of the prophet Isaiah to himself: "He has anointed me to bring good news to the poor. He has sent me to proclaim release to the captives and recovery of sight to the blind, to let the oppressed go free" (Luke 4:18). In other words, Jesus inaugurates the kingdom extolled by his mother before his birth.

Mary concludes her song by recalling God's mercy in liberating her people. Here she represents her people Israel, who long for freedom. She also sings on behalf of the Church, for all yearning for the coming of the reign of God.

Mary was instrumental in retrieving humanity from Satan's grip and ushering in God's kingdom of peace and justice. In her own time and way, so was Julie, whom people called "the walking love of God."

Response

The gap between the wealthy and the poor is widening. Figure out how to use your time, treasure, or talent to alleviate the suffering of the poor and further God's kingdom. Then get to work.

Saint Justin Martyr

c. 100–165 • Layman, Martyr • June 1

LIFE

Born in Judea, Saint Justin travelled to various schools, searching for truth. After studying philosophy, he met someone who introduced him to the Old Testament prophets. As a result, Justin became a Christian around age thirty and began to preach the faith and defend it in writing. He wrote two explanations of the Christian faith for Roman emperors. These works, called *Apologies*, have come down to us today. Justin opened a school in Rome during the time of Christian persecutions. As he expected, he was arrested along with six companions. At one point the Roman prefect threatened him with torture if he wouldn't sacrifice to idols. That is when he uttered his last words. Justin was then beheaded, earning the name Saint Justin Martyr.

LAST WORDS

*We hope to suffer torment
for the sake of our Lord Jesus Christ
and so be saved.*

Reflection: Martyrdom, Red and White

More believers were martyred in the last century than all other centuries combined. A martyr, from the Greek word meaning witness, is a believer who witnesses to the faith by giving up his or her life. All martyrs were honored as saints during the first centuries of the Church before canonization, the official process for declaring sainthood, was in place. Today two miracles resulting from the intercession of a candidate for canonization are required as "proof" that he or she is a citizen of heaven. For the canonization of a martyr, however, no miracles are necessary.

We are not inclined to look forward to martyrdom as joyfully as the early Christians, but would prefer to live. Take heart. There are two kinds of martyrdom, red, which is physical death, and white, which is dying to self. When persecutions ceased, some Christians decided to prove their faith by white martyrdom, leaving "the world," praying, and doing penance in the desert as monks and hermits.

White martyrdom has other forms. It is lived by the faithful who suffer emotionally. Some exhibit extraordinary love at the expense of their own comfort. These include a mother who patiently cares for her mentally disabled child year after year, a father who steadfastly holds down a challenging job to support his family, a teenager who is mocked for going to Mass and living by Catholic values, and a wife who stays with her sick and complaining husband although her children call her a fool. All of these people are suffering because of their faithful love. They may not be canonized but they certainly deserve a box seat in heaven.

The trials and pain of red and white martyrdom alike are the bricks and mortar of the kingdom of God. Moreover they clinch the salvation that Saint Justin was assured of through his suffering.

Response

How has your daily life offered opportunities to practice white martyrdom? In some way this week exercise love for God or neighbor even though it may hurt you.

St. Kateri
Tekakwitha

Jesus, I love you.

Saint Kateri Tekakwitha

1656–1680 • Virgin • July 14

LIFE

Saint Kateri was born in Ossernenon, a Mohawk village in New York where the Jesuit priest Isaac Jogues and his companions, lay brothers Jean de Lalande, and René Goupil, had been martyred years earlier. When she was four years old, her parents died in a smallpox epidemic. Kateri suffered the effects of the disease: poor vision and facial scarring. She was raised by her mother's Christian friend until the friend joined other Christians in Canada. When Kateri's uncle took custody of her, she was pressured to marry, but she professed loved only for the Great Spirit. After her Baptism, Kateri was persecuted for two years by other members of her tribe before escaping to Canada. There she went to daily Mass, cared for the sick, and taught children. When her short life ended, her scars vanished. Kateri is known as the Lily of the Mohawks.

LAST WORDS

Jesus, I love you.

Reflection: Loving God Back

To God, everyone is family. God, who is absolute love, created us out of love, intending that we receive and radiate his life and love forever. If that weren't astounding enough, after humankind foolishly shattered friendship with him, he sent his Son to repair it. And Jesus loved us to death. Every day our creator lavishes his love on us in ways known and unknown. And, incredibly, the almighty and self-sufficient God longs that we mortals love him in return. He even demands it. When Jesus was asked to name the greatest commandment, he replied without hesitation, "You shall love the Lord your God with all your heart, and with all your soul, and with all your mind" (Matthew 22:37).

We show our love by actions, such as giving gifts, doing favors, and making sacrifices. But that is not sufficient. Ask any girl who desperately yearns for the day when her boyfriend professes his love aloud to her. We do not have to wait to hear God say "I love you." God clearly and profusely declares his love for us. For example, God states, "You are precious in my sight, and honored, and I love you" (Isaiah 43:4). We also read, "For the mountains may depart and the hills be removed, but my steadfast love shall not depart from you" (Isaiah 54:10). And again, "I have loved you with an everlasting love" (Jeremiah 31:3). Jesus says, "As the Father has loved me, so I have loved you; abide in my love" (John 15:9).

The most potent words we can utter to God is a heartfelt "I love you." We can do this in a prayer attributed to Saint Francis Xavier. It begins, "O God, I love you for yourself and not that I may heaven gain" and ends, "I will love you, solely because you are my God and my eternal king."

Saint Kateri's love for God compelled her to act in ways unexpected of an Mohawk maiden. With her dying breath, as she had done countless times before, Kateri murmured, "Jesus, I love you," the perfect closing words to the beautiful love letter of her life.

Response

Did you ever have the awkward experience of saying "I love you" to someone who didn't say it back? Spare God this pain! Tell God you love him. Pray the traditional Act of Love on page 220 or another prayer, or profess your love in your own words.

Saint Lawrence

?–c. 258 • Deacon, Martyr • August 10

Life

Saint Lawrence, a deacon in Rome and the Church treasurer, sold sacred items and distributed the money to the poor after Pope Sixtus II and four deacons were executed during a persecution. When a government official demanded that Lawrence turn over the Church funds in three days, the deacon gathered the lepers, orphans, blind, and lame and presented them to the official, proclaiming, "These are the treasure of the Church." Lawrence was sentenced to die by fire on a huge grill.

Last Words

My flesh is well cooked on one side.
Turn the other and eat.

REFLECTION: THE GIFT OF LAUGHTER

Soon after Pope Francis was elected, he appeared sporting a red clown nose to congratulate a newlywed couple who were involved in clown ministry. Repeatedly this pope has reminded us that religion is a joyful affair. Joy has been called "carbonated holiness." It's little wonder, then, that Saint Lawrence, a very holy man, seems to crack a joke even in the throes of a painful death. Laughter, known as the best medicine, is even prescribed in Scripture: "A cheerful heart is good medicine, but a downcast spirit dries up the bones" (Proverbs 17:22). Jesuit Pierre Teilhard de Chardin claimed, "Joy is the infallible sign of the presence of God." Joy is one of the fruits of the Holy Spirit, the result of God's work in us.

God evidently has a sense of humor. Consider the practical jokes God played on his people. For example, when Sarah, Abraham's wife, was well past childbearing years, God made her a mother. Later, God handpicked Moses, a murderer with a speech impediment, to be the one to lead the Hebrews and persuade the Pharaoh to free his slaves. Similarly, Saul, a fierce persecutor of Christians, was en route to Damascus to capture Christians when God transformed him into Paul, one of the greatest apostles.

God's Son, Jesus, was not above engaging in some playfulness. He compared a rich person entering heaven to a camel squeezing through the eye of a needle. Another time, Jesus, no doubt with a twinkle in his eye, sent Peter, an experienced fisherman, to fish for tax money carried in a fish's mouth. Bantering with a Gentile woman, Jesus so delighted in her clever riposte that he changed his mind and cured her daughter.

The prince in Antoine de St. Exupery's *The Little Prince* left his friend the gift of his laughter. We Christians must teach the world how to laugh again. In the strength of our faith, with the ideal woman of Proverbs 31:25, we can "laugh at the times to come." In fact, we can die in the footsteps of Lawrence, enjoying the last laugh in more ways than one.

RESPONSE

How do you feel when you've had a good laugh? Give someone the gift of laughter. Send a funny card, tell a joke, or play a harmless prank.

Saint Lawrence Ruiz

c. 1600–1637 • Layman, Martyr • September 28

LIFE

Saint Lawrence, the son of a Chinese father and a Filipino mother, lived in Manila. Married with two sons and a daughter, he was a calligrapher by trade. When he was implicated in a murder, he boarded a ship with missionaries to avoid arrest. He soon learned the missionaries were headed for Japan where Catholics were being persecuted. There, along with his companions, Lawrence was arrested and imprisoned for two years. During his trial, he asked if he would be freed if he gave up the faith. Receiving no clear answer, he declared, "I am a Christian. I shall die for God." He was tortured and hung by his feet over a pit until he died two days later.

LAST WORDS

If I had a thousand lives,
I would offer them to God.

Reflection: Offering Our Lives

In one of her poems, Mary Oliver poses a thought-provoking question: "Tell me, what is it you plan to do with your one wild and precious life?" From our first breath to our last, we are privileged to bask in the love of family and friends, soak up the wonders of creation, and exploit our talents.

We are so full of potential. We can squander our life, ruin it, or as Saint Teresa of Calcutta advised, shape it into something beautiful for God. We can return our life to the Giver by praying the Morning Offering, consecrating all the aspects of the day ahead. We can also offer ourselves to God at Mass during the preparation of gifts. The bread and wine and the donations brought to the altar are symbols of our life and our work.

A few courageous people make the supreme sacrifice and cut their lives short for love of others. In Charles Dickens's classic novel *A Tale of Two Cities*, Sydney Carton passionately loves Lucie Manette. This love compels him to switch places with her husband who is to be executed by guillotine. In real life men and women in the armed forces lay down their lives so others can live freely. For love of God, Saint Lawrence surrendered his one life. In a fervent outburst, he avowed that, if he had 1,000 lives, he was willing to offer every one of them.

Some people might accuse Lawrence of wasting his life. They couldn't be more wrong. He used his life as extravagantly as the woman in the gospels who expressed her love for Jesus by breaking open an alabaster jar and spilling out her expensive ointment for him. In his sacrifice, Lawrence had only his life to give, following the example of the Son of God, who willingly gave his life because of his love for the Father...and us.

Response

For whom or what would you give your life? Promise to live every day for God. Start each day by praying the Morning Offering. See page 220.

Saint Louis de Montfort

1673–1716 • Priest, Confessor, Founder • April 28

LIFE

Born in France, Saint Louis was ordained a priest and then became a Third Order Dominican. He was devoted to the poor and practiced voluntary poverty. Commissioned Apostolic Missionary in France by Pope Clement XI, he preached the Gospel in countless missions in towns and villages. His teachings influenced four popes and helped shape Marian theology. He also founded three religious congregations. His books, especially *True Devotion Mary* and *The Secret of the Rosary*, are still read today. His dying words were a rebuke of Satan.

LAST WORDS

In vain do you attack me;
I am between Jesus and Mary.
I have finished my course: all is over.
I shall sin no more.

Reflection: Satan and Temptation

In a bus on the way to a convention, I shared some overwhelming problems I was experiencing in carrying out my ministry with the person sharing my seat. She responded, "You are doing so much good. Satan must hate you." I was taken aback by her statement. We modern people seldom think of Satan, except when he appears in a horror movie, and some people do not consider him a real person. *The Catechism of the Catholic Church* describes Satan as a pure spirit, a creature who rebelled against God and is responsible for infecting God's good universe with sin and evil. Jesus, like his peers, believed in devils, or demons. In the gospels he speaks to them, is tempted by them, and casts them out of the possessed. Satanists not only believe in the devil but worship him.

According to tradition, demons resent us for taking their places in heaven, and they are relentless in trying to prevent us from doing so by luring us away from what is good. They hope to get revenge on God by depriving us of eternal bliss. Scripture warns, "Like a roaring lion your adversary the devil prowls around, looking for someone to devour" (1 Peter 5:8).

Saint Louis proved victorious in his struggle against Satan. A statue in Saint Peter's Basilica in Rome depicts him crushing a serpent, a symbol of Satan. The Blessed Virgin Mary is also portrayed stepping on a serpent to show that her son once and for all conquered Satan, wresting us from his clutches and freeing us from sin and death. At our Baptism we renounce Satan and evil works. A hedonistic and materialistic culture, peer pressure, and our own weakened nature make it difficult, but not impossible, to resist sin. Through the grace Jesus won for us, we can be faithful to our baptismal vows. We too can crush Satan.

Response

The Book of Revelation recounts that Saint Michael the Archangel led the good angels to victory over the rebellious ones. When you are being tempted, pray to him for help. Also ask Saint Michael to defend the Church.

Saint Margaret Clitherow

1556–1586 • Laywoman, Martyr • March 26

LIFE

Saint Margaret, known as the Pearl of York, lived in England at a time when it was a crime to practice the Catholic faith. Marrying at age fifteen, she became a Catholic at age eighteen, while her husband remained a Protestant. She offered her home for the secret celebration of Mass and harbored priests, a crime that led to her arrest. To spare her three children from testifying and being tortured, she refused a trial. On March 25, Good Friday, Margaret was crushed to death between the door of her house and a sharp rock. Her daughter became a religious sister and her two sons, priests.

LAST WORDS

Jesu! Jesu! Jesu!
Have mercy on me!

Reflection: Jesus, Font of Mercy

Mercy is central to our faith. Pope Francis declared an Extraordinary Year of Mercy that began on December 8, 2015. Previously, in 2002, Pope Saint John Paul II made the Sunday after Easter a universal feast celebrating Divine Mercy. Devotion to Jesus under this title originated with Saint Faustina Kowalska, a Polish nun who frequently spoke to Jesus and recorded their conversations in a diary.

In 1931, Jesus, robed in white and with his right hand raised in blessing, appeared to Faustina. His left hand touched his heart from which emanated red and white rays, representing the blood and water that flowed from his side when the soldier pierced his body with a lance. Jesus directed Faustina to have this vision rendered as a painting along with the words, "Jesus, I trust in you." The Divine Mercy Devotion exhorts us to extend mercy to others in action, word, and prayer.

Faustina said that Jesus instructed her to "proclaim that mercy, not omnipotence or justice, is the greatest attribute of God." This echoes Psalm 145:8-9, "The LORD is gracious and merciful, slow to anger…his compassion is over all that he has made." On Calvary Jesus revealed the depth of his mercy by redeeming us at great personal cost, the price of his blood. He promised Faustina that anyone who trusted in his mercy would receive it, no exceptions. We only need to trust in his mercy to have our sins erased from the record of our lives. In her last words, Saint Margaret may have appealed to Jesus for mercy and forgiveness for her sins, however small, or for release from the excruciating pain she endured for fifteen minutes before meeting her redeemer face-to-face.

Response

The Sacrament of Penance is the channel through which the mercy of Jesus flows to us. Celebrate it soon, and thank Jesus for the forgiveness he offers you.

Saint Margaret Mary Alacoque

1647–1690 • Virgin, Religious • October 16

LIFE

Saint Margaret Mary, born in France, lost her father when she was only eight years old and, with her family, fell into poverty. After being cured of an illness by the Blessed Virgin, Margaret Mary became a Visitation nun at the convent of Paray-le-Monial. Working in the infirmary, she was known for her kindness rather than her skill. For two years Jesus appeared to her, entreating her to tell everyone to love his Sacred Heart and promising blessings to those who received Communion on the first Friday of each month. Saint Claude de la Colombiere, a Jesuit, was Margaret Mary's ally in promoting devotion to the Sacred Heart in the face of opposition from theologians and members of her own community who doubted the authenticity of her visions.

LAST WORDS

*I need nothing but God
and to lose myself in the heart of Jesus.*

Reflection: The Sacred Heart of Jesus

Hundreds of churches are named in honor of the Sacred Heart of Jesus. The Solemnity of the Sacred Heart is celebrated on the Friday nineteen days after Pentecost, and the month of June is dedicated to the Sacred Heart. Devotees pray the novena and litany to the Sacred Heart and wear Sacred Heart scapulars and badges. Families consecrated to the Sacred Heart enthrone an image of him in their homes.

The heart of Jesus is a powerful, trifold symbol. First, in our culture a heart represents our whole being. When we say, "I love you with all my heart," we mean "with all that I am." Second, the heart, which keeps us alive by beating roughly 100,800 times a day, signifies life. And third, the heart is a symbol of love. The heart of Jesus then represents the whole God-Man, his life, and his tremendous love for us.

Love compelled God to hide his divinity and become one of his creatures, demonstrating with his whole being that he cares for us. Jesus' earthly life ended with the ultimate act of love: dying for the beloved. After Jesus died on the cross, a soldier, traditionally known as Longinus, thrust a lance into his side, piercing his heart. This event is all the more reason to view the heart as a fitting symbol for the love of Jesus.

In art the Sacred Heart is surmounted by symbols of love: a cross encircled with thorns and flames shooting forth from the heart to represent the burning love Jesus has for us. Some artists have depicted Jesus offering his heart to us. At one point, Jesus lamented to Saint Margaret Mary, "Behold this heart, which has so loved men [and women], but which is so little loved in return." Unrequited love is sad. Unrequited divine love is terrible.

Lovers do not care where they are or what they are doing as long as they are in each other's presence. Margaret Mary knew that the one thing necessary was to be lost in the heart of Jesus. Her sole wish was to be one with Jesus. That wish would be fulfilled.

Response

What evidence have you been given recently that God loves you? Spend a few minutes in silence becoming more aware of God beholding you and loving you right now just as you are.

Saint Margaret of Scotland

1046–1093 • Laywoman • November 16

LIFE

Although Saint Margaret was of English nobility, she was born in Hungary. One day as the family was returning to England, a storm blew the ship off course to Scotland, where she married King Malcolm III and and bore eight children. Margaret, a woman of prayer and penance, was devoted to the people in her realm. She fed the poor every day, washed their feet, and set up hospitals for them. Margaret died four days after King Malcolm and the couple's oldest son were killed in battle. Her last words were the Prayers before Communion from a missal.

LAST WORDS

O Lord Jesus Christ, who by thy death hast given life to the world, deliver me.

Reflection: Redemption

After the death of Jesus in Mel Gibson's *The Passion of the Christ*, a hideous being representing the defeated Satan/evil screams long and loud. This disturbing image has power to jolt viewers into a new realization of what Jesus accomplished. We who have heard the story of our redemption all our lives may have become immune to its earthshaking significance.

Consider what our plight would be if Jesus had not come. Our lives on earth would be devoid of purpose and hope. We would be doomed to live forever in hell with creatures consumed with hate for one another and us. At best we would anticipate obliteration or at least a shadowy existence in a nebulous afterlife. We would never know the joy of living forever, enjoying the God who made us and enveloped by his love. All our loved ones would face the same sad end.

Jesus prevented this dreadful scenario by stitching up the wound caused by Adam and Eve. This is what we celebrate every year during Holy Week and Easter and at every Eucharist. Because Jesus died and rose, we can share divine life as God's beloved children. We are blessed with a future in which we can live in unending joy with glorified bodies like that of the risen Lord. Jesus has delivered us from evil and will deliver us into heaven—if we, like Saint Margaret, live a life full of love. Alleluia!

Response

Saints are happy in the knowledge that they are saved and have the hope of eternal bliss. Let your smile, cheerfulness, and optimism reflect the fact that you are redeemed.

St. Maria Goretti

I want him to be with me in Paradise.
May God forgive him
because I already have forgiven him.

Saint Maria Goretti

1890–1902 • Virgin, Martyr • July 6

LIFE

Saint Maria's poor family labored on another man's farm, sharing their home with another worker and his eighteen-year-old son Alessandro. After sexually harassing Maria for some time, Alessandro found the eleven-year-old Maria home alone one day and tried to force her to sin. When Maria repulsed him, he stabbed her fourteen times. She lived for twenty-four hours. Alessandro, who was sentenced to thirty years in prison, repented after dreaming that Maria handed him fourteen lilies, which turned into flames. After serving twenty-seven years, Alessandro was released and entered a monastery. He even attended Maria's canonization. Maria's final words referred to her murderer.

LAST WORDS

I want him to be with me in Paradise.
May God forgive him
because I already have forgiven him.

Reflection: Forgiveness

Author C.S. Lewis noted, "Everyone says that forgiveness is a lovely idea until he has something to forgive." Forgiving someone is one of the most difficult things we can do. Our strong sense of justice makes us more comfortable with the moral code "an eye for an eye and a tooth for a tooth." When a person betrays us, insults us, steals from us, speaks ill of us to others, or disappoints us, our first instinct is to lash out. Our wound seems to demand that we retaliate by inflicting injury on the one who harmed us. We feel like cursing our enemy.

Jesus declaws this natural urge. He expects us, his followers, to love our enemies. He taught us to forgive someone seventy-times seven, which is a Jewish way of saying every single time. Saint Maria may have been illiterate, but she knew Jesus and certainly took his words concerning forgiveness to heart. She forgave Alessandro and even wished him the best—precisely, eternal happiness in heaven. If a young girl could forgive her killer, if Jesus could forgive his executioners, and if God can forgive us time and time again, surely we can summon the strength to forgive those who offend us.

We also need to forgive ourselves, for at times we are our own worst enemy. Our egos like to imagine that we are perfect, and it irks us when we do things we regret. But to constantly brood over lapses and mentally whip ourselves for them is not only unhealthy but unholy. Forgiveness of self and others sets us free. When we forgive, we exercise the divine quality of mercy. We can also actually look forward to God answering our daring prayer "forgive us our trespasses as we forgive those who trespass against us."

Response

Who needs your forgiveness? Before going to bed, forgive them or at least pray for the grace to forgive them.

Saint Martin of Tours

c. 316–397 • Bishop • November 11

LIFE

Born the son of a Roman army officer in Hungary, Saint Martin moved to Italy with his family. When he was ten, he began attending Christian churches and, against his parents' wishes, became a catechumen. At age fifteen he joined the army. A legend has it that he once divided his cloak with a beggar. That night in a dream Christ appeared wearing the half-cloak. After his baptism, Martin resigned from the army and became a soldier for Christ. He converted his mother, fought false teachings, and for about ten years went out to preach the Gospel while living in a hermitage that later became a monastery. Then to his chagrin, the people of Tours acclaimed him their bishop. Martin freed prisoners, founded a famous monastery, and was the first to form parishes.

LAST WORDS

Lord, if your people still need me,
I do not refuse the work. Your will be done.

An old story tells of three men chopping away at rocks. When asked what they were doing, one man replied, "I'm cutting stone." Another man said, "I'm earning a living." The third man proclaimed, "I am building a cathedral." Work means different things to different people. To Saint Martin, who labored diligently for the Lord, it was a way to love and serve God. Even as an old man, he was willing to keep working as long as God wished for the sake of God's people.

Ordained men, vowed religious, and lay ministers work for God full time. But every church member's job description includes building the kingdom of God. We have the mandate to carry on the work of Christ in the places and circumstances of our lives, with the people we encounter regularly at home or work as well as those we meet infrequently or by chance. Who will build the kingdom if we neglect this crucial task?

As the hub of Christian life, the parish offers multiple opportunities for promoting God's kingdom. We can assist at liturgy, for example, by being a lector, usher, or choir member. (By the way, *liturgy* means the public work of the Church.) We can be active on parish committees, participate in service projects, and volunteer our talents for parish needs like gardening, painting, and helping with technology.

If our daily job is not directly church-related, it can still be kingdom-related. Whatever we do somehow contributes to the building up of humankind. In addition, we can carry out our tasks "for the greater honor and glory of God." As Paul exhorted the first Christians, "Whatever you do, in word or deed, do everything in the name of the Lord Jesus, giving thanks to God the Father through him" (Colossians 3:17). Let our aim be that when our work on earth is completed, we hear God say, as surely he greeted Martin, "Well done, good and faithful servant."

RESPONSE

How do you contribute to the kingdom by carrying out your particular job? Strive to work with your whole heart, keeping in mind the advice: "Ask God's blessing on your work but don't ask him to do it for you."

Saint Mary Magdalene de Pazzi

1566–1607 • Virgin, Religious, Mystic • May 25

LIFE

Born to a wealthy family in Florence, Italy, Saint Mary Magdalene entered a Carmelite convent at age sixteen. For most of her life, she experienced spiritual gifts. She became superior of her community and urged the pope and other bishops to reform the Church. For five years she experienced the mental suffering of depression and temptations. Then for three years before her death, she endured physical suffering in the form of a painful disease. By living according to her motto—"to suffer, not to die"—she taught the value of redemptive suffering. Her dying words were addressed to the sisters of her religious community .

LAST WORDS

The last thing I ask of you is that you love Jesus alone, that you trust him completely and that you encourage one another continually to suffer for the love of him.

Reflection: Suffering

A priest once compared suffering to garbage. While both are usually considered useless, they actually store potential energy accessible to those who know how to tap it. We are often puzzled by the reason for suffering. We blame original sin for introducing suffering, but we believe that God ardently loves us and regards us as his children. Does a good Father stand by and let his children suffer? Many people have tackled the age-old mystery of suffering, but not even the Bible gives us an inkling of an answer. When the innocent Job dares to ask God the reason for his extreme suffering, he is only reminded in no uncertain terms that God is in charge of the universe. Who is he, a mere mortal, to question the Immortal One?

At first glance, Saint Mary Magdalene might be judged a masochist. She was able to thrive through her suffering because she possessed the Christian key to coping with it. Jesus taught that only by losing our life would we find it. In becoming "the suffering servant," Jesus helps us find meaning in our pains and heartaches. By uniting our suffering with the passion and death of Jesus, we can transform it into a powerful source of grace. Our suffering can contribute to the salvation of the world and further God's reign. Enduring suffering with patience is one way of taking up our cross. It is also an opportunity to "offer it up" for a specific intention. Mary Magdalene used her suffering especially to benefit the poor souls in purgatory.

Suffering can be wasted or mined for its riches. It can make us bitter or better. The choice is ours.

Response

Archbishop Fulton J. Sheen said, "Nothing is worse than wasted suffering." Are you currently suffering in some way? If so, attach a good intention to it and make it fruitful.

Saint Monica

c. 322–387 • Widow • August 27

LIFE

Saint Monica, a Christian in North Africa, was married to Patricius, a pagan official. She patiently bore his temper and bad habits as well as the antipathy of his mother. In time, Patricius became a Christian, and his mother was won over by Monica's forgiveness. Augustine, one of Monica's three sons, caused her much grief because of his rejection of Christianity and his immoral life. She prayed and fasted for him and followed him to Italy. In Milan, Saint Ambrose, her spiritual director, told her, "Surely the son of so many tears will not perish." In fact, Ambrose converted Augustine. Monica died as she and her son journeyed back to Africa. Her last words were spoken to him.

LAST WORDS

Lay this body anywhere, and take no trouble over it. One thing only do I ask of you, that you remember me at the altar of the Lord wherever you may be.

Reflection: Remembering Deceased Loved Ones

When I was editor of a religion series, I received a call from a Jewish co-worker who wanted to know how to spell *poor souls*. Was it *pore* souls, *pour* souls, or *poor* souls? My friend, a monsignor who was a censor of the books, preferred the term *holy souls* for those people who were in the waiting room of heaven undergoing purification to make them more worthy to be in the presence of the all-holy God.

Why do we pray for the dead? The scriptural basis is 2 Maccabees 12:43-45 where Judas Maccabeus has a sacrifice offered for his fallen soldiers, giving witness to his belief in the resurrection and in the holy duty of praying for the dead. In 1563, the Council of Trent, in confirming the existence of purgatory, attested to the need for this practice.

Like Judas Maccabeus, we believe our beloved departed ones still exist and will rise at the end of the world. Bound together in the Communion of Saints, the family of God, we pray for one another. As a matter of fact, we dedicate the whole month of November to the poor souls, with the high point being November 2, the Feast of All Souls. In addition, it is our tradition to pray, "Eternal rest grant unto them, O Lord, and let perpetual light shine upon them. May they rest in peace."

The most perfect and logical way to pray for the deceased is at Mass. We say farewell to a loved one at a funeral Mass that focuses on resurrection. At every Mass, as the saving acts of Jesus are represented, we ask for the graces he won to be applied to our family members and friends who have gone before us. At the end of the Eucharistic Prayer, as the priest prays a commemoration for the dead, we can recall those for whom we wish to pray.

Well aware of the power of the Eucharist, Saint Monica asked her son Augustine, a bishop, to remember her at every Mass he offered. Since all members of Christ's body, living and dead, are united in the Eucharist, we can say that Monica, as a saint in heaven, worshipped God with her son.

Response

In what ways do you remember your deceased loved ones? During the commemoration of the dead at Mass, make it a point to call to mind people you know who have died.

Saint Paschal Baylon

1540–1592 • Mystic, Religious • May 17

Life

Saint Paschal, the son of poor peasants in Spain, was a shepherd as a youth. He taught himself to read and became a man of profound and often ecstatic prayer. In obedience to a vision, he joined a Franciscan order as a brother. Once, as he carried a message to France, he was attacked by heretics for defending the dogma of the Real Presence. Paschal is known for his extraordinary devotion to the Blessed Sacrament. He was born and died on Pentecost.

Last Words

Jesus. Jesus.

Reflection: The Blessed Sacrament

We might envy those first-century men and women who were privileged to see and hear Jesus in the flesh, but out of deep love for us, Jesus made it possible for him to be with every generation, including our own, through the institution of the Blessed Sacrament. Some Christians hold that the sacred bread and wine are merely symbols of Christ. We Catholics, however, believe in the Real Presence, that Jesus is actually with us under the forms of bread and wine. At the Eucharist when we consume a piece of sacred bread and take a sip of sacred wine, Jesus enters us and unites us with himself. This miracle is mind-boggling. Not only did God stoop to become a human being, but, as if that weren't enough, God assumes the guise of inanimate objects, bread and wine.

When we come before the tabernacle in church, we are in the presence of Jesus. Just as the sun tans our skin without any effort on our part, Jesus in the Blessed Sacrament can effect a change in us. He can make us holier, more like himself. Did you ever notice that loving couples celebrating fifty or more years of marriage tend to resemble each other?

When Saint John Vianney asked an old man who spent long hours before the Blessed Sacrament what he did, the man replied, "I look at him and he looks at me." Words are not necessary between people in love.

When Saint John Neumann was bishop of Philadelphia, he introduced the Forty Hours Devotion. This is the practice of having the Blessed Sacrament exposed for adoration for forty hours once a year. Some churches have reduced the time for this practice, while others have perpetual adoration. Saint Paschal spent much of his life, sometimes the entire night, with the Blessed Sacrament. By communing with Jesus, he grew in his knowledge and love of Jesus and consequently became a humble, loving saint. His last words echoed what he had been repeating his entire life, the name of his beloved.

Response

How firm is your belief that Jesus is present in the Blessed Sacrament? Steal some time to be with him. Come early to Mass or remain afterwards, participate in Benediction or Eucharistic Adoration, or make a visit to a church or chapel.

Saint Paulinus of Nola

c. 354–431 • Bishop • June 22

Life

Born in France, Saint Paulinus became the governor of an Italian town. He was baptized after marrying Therasia, a wealthy Spanish Christian. Their only child, a son, lived only eight days. The couple donated their wealth to the poor. Impressed by the Christian lifestyle of Paulinus, the town's inhabitants persuaded him to become a priest. After Therasia died, Paulinus became bishop of Nola, where he sheltered the homeless on the first floor of his house. His prolific writings included poems and correspondence with several other saints. He uttered his last words as the lamps were lighted for Vespers.

Last Words

I have prepared a lamp for my Christ.

REFLECTION: WORKS OF MERCY

Jesus told the parable of the ten bridesmaids to encourage us to be ready for his Second Coming, but we can also apply it to being prepared for death. In the parable ten bridesmaids, all carrying oil lamps, wait for the arrival of the bridegroom. When his approach is announced, five bridesmaids, realizing they lack sufficient oil to escort the wedding procession, depart to purchase some more. When the bridegroom arrives, they are gone, and when they return, they are refused entrance to the wedding feast. The oil symbolizes the good deeds that are necessary to pass through heaven's gates and join in the wedding feast of heaven where Jesus, the bridegroom, presides.

The lamp of Saint Paulinus, fueled by his abundance of good deeds, shone brightly, guaranteeing that Jesus would welcome him into heaven. Good deeds, or works of mercy, are like a passport for entrance into the kingdom of God. Jesus made this crystal clear when he enumerated the corporal works of mercy: feed the hungry, give drink to the thirsty, clothe the naked, shelter the homeless, and visit the sick and imprisoned. (See Matthew 25:31-46.) The work of mercy of burying the dead was added later. The spiritual works of mercy, which can be traced back to a catechism written by Paulinus' friend Saint Augustine, are admonish the sinner, instruct the ignorant, counsel the doubtful, comfort the sorrowful, bear wrongs patiently, and forgive all injuries. All of these holy works are ways of serving others. Sadly, as Archbishop Fulton J. Sheen observed, "Although we have Jesus' example of the washing of the apostles' feet as a model of service, it is difficult to find people today fighting for the towel."

We encounter people in need of a helping hand or a kind heart in our communities,and in our own families. Some in foreign lands are also suffering. By reaching out to them with compassion, we imitate the all-merciful One, who always responded to the cries of the poor. When we, like Paulinus, perform works of mercy, our light shines brilliantly, warming and illuminating the world. The gates of heaven will one day swing open wide for us.

RESPONSE

Check your oil supply. Which works of mercy have you performed lately? Which ones need more attention?

Saint Paul Miki

c. 1564–1597 • Martyr, Religious • February 6

Life

Saint Paul Miki, born into a noble Japanese family, became a Jesuit brother and completed his studies for the priesthood. Before he could be ordained, he was arrested with twenty-five others during a persecution of Christians. After being tortured, the condemned men walked for more than 300 miles, preaching and praying along the way. On a hill in Nagasaki they were affixed to crosses with iron bands. An outstanding preacher, Paul even preached from his cross before all of the condemned were thrust through with lances.

Last Words

After Christ's example I forgive my persecutors. I do not hate them. I ask God to have pity on all, and I hope my blood will fall on my fellow men as a fruitful rain.

Reflection: The Power of Example

A priest explained that he owed his vocation to his father. Every morning, no matter what the weather, his dad would rise extra early to go to Mass before starting work. This example sent a strong message to the boy about the value of faith, so much so that he decided to dedicate his life to serving the Church.

Teens in particular are susceptible to peer pressure, dressing and acting to fit in with their friends. Some of us may try to imitate movie and rock stars, heroes, and even our neighbors. And we can exert a power over others by our example—positive or negative. A single person, taking the first step in a good or heroic work, can trigger a domino effect of good deeds, spurring the hesitant to join in. Think of the response to someone who is drowning, trapped in a burning car, or being harassed for their religious beliefs. If we step up, others may follow our lead. If we model faith and integrity, who knows how many lives we will touch and transform?

Saint Paul preached not only with words but with his blood. His wish that his blood be like fruitful rain is reminiscent of the second-century theologian Tertullian's claim, "The blood of martyrs is the seed of the Church." This figure of speech expresses the belief that a martyr's sacrifice will produce a crop of new Christians. Paul hoped only the best for his persecutors and fellowmen—that they would be inspired to come to believe in Jesus. His wish was granted: The Church in Japan survived underground for a remarkable 300 years.

Response

Whose faith has helped to nurture and deepen your own? Thank God for this person or persons.

Saint Perpetua

?–c. 203 • Martyr • March 7

Life

Saint Perpetua lived during the persecution of Christians in Carthage, Africa. The mother of an infant, she was a catechumen when she was arrested along with four others preparing for Baptism, including Felicity, her pregnant slave. Perpetua's father pleaded with her to gain her freedom by sacrificing to the pagan gods, but she refused. In prison, the catechumens were baptized. On a national holiday, they were led into an arena before a jeering crowd. When a mad heifer failed to kill Perpetua and Felicity, the two women were beheaded. Perpetua's last words were addressed to her brother and a catechumen in the crowd.

Last Words

Stand firm in the faith and love one another,
and do not be weakened
by what we have gone through.

Reflection: Love

In Charles Schultz's comic strip *Peanuts*, Linus once announced, "I love mankind. It's people I can't stand." Linus knew from experience how difficult it can be to love, especially with a big sister like Lucy.

Awaiting her death, Saint Perpetua echoed Jesus' last words to the apostles on the night before he died: "Love one another as I have loved you" (John 15:12). Jesus told his first followers that everyone would identify them as his disciples if they loved one another. (See John 13:35.) Love was to be the hallmark, the characteristic trait of Christians. As a hymn reminds us, "They will know we are Christians by our love."

Jesus stated that the greatest commandment was to love God. The second greatest was to love our neighbor as ourselves. (See Mark 12:29-31.) We show love for God by holding fast to the faith in the face of persecution or temptation and by trying to please him. We show love for others by following the last seven of the Ten Commandments. Jesus set the bar for love high, requiring that instead of despising our enemies and persecutors, we are to love them and pray for them, a feat comparable to hugging a porcupine.

It's said that in his old age, the apostle John uttered no more than, "Children, love one another." Why is love so great? Because God is defined as love. John wrote in a letter, "God is love" (1 John 4:8), words Pope Benedict XVI chose as the title for his first encyclical. It follows that the more we love, the more we are like God and the more deserving we are of God's love.

Our very existence is the result of love, God's love and the love between our parents. Our destiny is to embrace and be embraced by Love without end. According to Saint John of the Cross, we will be judged on love. No doubt, Perpetua had nothing to worry about.

Response

Praying for people we do not like can soften our hearts toward them. Say a prayer for someone who has hurt you in a way that is hard to forgive and forget.

Saint Peter of Alcantara

1499–1562 • Religious, Priest • October 19

LIFE

Saint Peter, born to a noble family in Spain, joined a Franciscan community. He became a priest, a persuasive preacher, especially to the poor, and a superior in his order, but his attempts to reform his community were not welcomed. A man of deep prayer, Peter worked miracles and experienced ecstasies. Described as "an athlete of penance," he slept and ate little and practiced poverty. After living as a hermit for a while, Peter founded strict Franciscan communities. He was a spiritual director to Saint Teresa of Avila. His last words, the first verse of Psalm 122, were spoken as he knelt in prayer.

LAST WORDS

I was glad when they said to me,
"Let us go to the house of the LORD."

REFLECTION: CHURCHES

Someone remarked to a Catholic friend, "If I believed that God was in the tabernacle, I would crawl down the aisle on my knees!" We are so accustomed to our God living in our churches that we might forget what an incredible privilege we have been given.

The Israelites, our spiritual ancestors, also knew God's presence among them. They prayed the psalm verse quoted by Saint Peter on their way to worship at their magnificent Temple. King Solomon built this Temple to house the Ark of the Covenant, the chest that God had Moses construct as God's dwelling place among his people.

Jesus acknowledged God's presence in the Temple when, at age twelve, he was missing for three days in Jerusalem. After his frantic parents found him in the Temple, he explained, "Did you not know I must be in my Father's house?" (Luke 2:41-52). And later when Jesus drove the money changers out of the Temple, he claimed they were making his Father's house a den of thieves.

The Temple in Jerusalem was the only house of God for the Jewish people, while each of our churches throughout the world is a house of God, from the grandiose Saint Peter's Basilica in Rome to the tiniest chapel. When we walk into a Catholic church, we come into the presence of God in the miracle of the Blessed Sacrament. The Israelites rejoiced as they went up to the Temple. We too ought to be overjoyed to encounter God in church, whether we are praising and thanking him in the Eucharist or spending quiet moments with him in personal prayer.

When Peter prayed his last words, he wasn't thinking of a Temple or a church but of heaven, the permanent house of God. He was looking forward to beholding God there face-to-face in the beatific vision.

RESPONSE

Renew your awareness of Jesus in the Blessed Sacrament. Bless yourself with holy water as you enter and leave church, genuflect or bow with reverence, and observe silence except during worship. When opportunity arises, teach children to behave in God's house with respect and reverence.

Saint Peter Chanel

1803–1841 • Religious, Priest, Martyr • April 28

LIFE

Born in France, Saint Peter was a shepherd as a child. He became a parish priest and spent three years reviving a parish, giving witness in a special way by his devotion to the sick. Wishing to serve as a missionary, Peter helped form the Society of Mary (Marists), whose focus was the missions, but then he obediently remained teaching at the seminary for five years. Eventually he and a Marist brother were sent to the South Pacific island of Fortuna, a place of great hardship. Few natives converted, and when the chief's son asked to be baptized, the angry chief sent his son-in-law, Musumusu, who had his warriors club Peter to death. In time, almost all the islanders, including Musumusu, became Catholic.

LAST WORDS

It is well for me.

REFLECTION: ACCEPTING GOD'S WILL

Someone in dire straits might wail, "I just want to die." It is perfectly understandable that Saint Peter might have welcomed death in the circumstances on Fortuna. Cannibalism was practiced, the language was almost impossible to learn, and Peter was plagued by heat, hunger, and exhaustion. Death would have been a relief. Yet, that is probably not what Peter meant when he greeted his death with "It is well for me."

Saint Ignatius, an expert in the spiritual life, taught holy indifference, that is, a total openness to God's will. That means accepting anything that God has mapped out for us whether we understand it or not, whether we like it or not. We make *God's* will *our* will. The Blessed Virgin Mary, who responded, "Let it be," to her daunting mission, is a model of this quality. So is her son, who during his agony before certain death prayed, "Not my will but yours be done." Surely Peter was indifferent to the direction of his life, having already placed himself completely in God's hands. He viewed death as a part of God's plan for him and embraced it as good and necessary.

Each time we pray the Our Father we ask, "Your will be done." Confident that God loves us and has our best interests at heart, we surrender to his will. We might see our lives as something resembling the underside of a piece of needlework, a mess of knots and crisscrossed threads, but from the vantage point of heaven we will realize that God was creating a work of beauty. Accepting God's will releases us from worry and bitterness. As the Italian poet Dante wrote, "In God's will is our peace."

RESPONSE

When has something that appeared at first to be negative turn out to be a blessing? Cultivate the habit of trusting our good God in all the twists and turns of life.

Saint Peter Verona

1206–1252 • Religious, Priest, Martyr • April 6

LIFE

Saint Peter, a Dominican priest and a gifted preacher, brought hundreds throughout Italy into the Catholic Church. Besides railing against being Catholic in name only, he denounced the heresy of Catharism and, for a brief time, was Inquisitor. Carino, an assassin hired by the Cathars, and another man attacked Saint Peter and his companion, striking Peter's head with an axe. As Peter died, he recited the first article of the Apostles' Creed. Legend holds that he wrote "I believe in God" on the ground with his blood. The amazing upshot of Peter's death was that Carino became a Dominican brother.

LAST WORDS

I believe in God, the Father almighty,
creator of heaven and earth.

Reflection: Evangelizing

A young boy was asked why he believed in God. After thinking a moment, the boy replied, "I guess it's something that runs in our family." True, we can divine that God exists from gazing at the stars, reading *National Geographic*, or watching nature programs on television, but most of us have inherited our faith. However and whenever it came, it is sheer gift. Down through the centuries, staunch believers like Peter protected the faith and handed it on. Now we in turn are responsible for preserving and sharing this treasure.

Recent popes have stressed the importance of evangelization, sharing the good news. In fact, Pope Saint John Paul II called bringing people to Jesus our *supreme* duty. Evangelization is the Church's essential task and the primary way we serve others. For too long we assumed our obligations as Catholics were to pay, pray, and obey. Now we are being reminded that we are also to *relay*. The first Christians were passionate about sharing Jesus with others—even when that passion led to their martyrdom. The renewed call to evangelization challenges us to live our faith with that same passion, enflaming us with the desire us to introduce others to Jesus for the first time and to invite back to him those who have strayed.

The most persuasive way to evangelize is by living by the values and principles of Jesus Christ. Legend attributes the following injunction to Saint Francis: "Preach the Gospel always. If necessary use words." We preach the faith in the workplace when we are people of integrity, when we are honest, when we walk away from damaging conversations, and when we aim for perfection. We preach the faith in our neighborhoods when we are kind, helpful, and generous. We preach the faith in our families when we pray, attend church together, love, and forgive. If we don't hand on the faith, who will?

Response

Evangelizing others presupposes that we ourselves have been evangelized. How well do you know God? Your Catholic faith? Evangelize yourself. Spend extra time praying, read Scripture and Catholic literature, browse Catholic websites, and attend lectures on the faith.

Saint Philip Neri

1515–1595 • Religious, Priest, Founder • May 26

Life

Saint Philip was dedicated to renewing the people of Rome, who were so impressed by his spirituality and sense of humor that they persuaded him to seek ordination. He was spiritual director for several saints and advised the clergy, including a pope. Some young men whom he led in assisting at hospitals and discussing spiritual topics eventually became his community, the Congregation of Priests of the Oratory. A humble and simple man, Philip refused the pope's offer to become a cardinal. As an act of humility prompted by people acclaiming him as a saint, he shaved off half of his beard! His final words were spoken after a day of hearing confessions and receiving visitors.

Last Words

Last of all, we must die.

REFLECTION: JOY

The proverb "Idleness is the devil's workshop" is quoted to spur us to action. Saint Philip, "the Apostle of Rome," was so busy that the devil would not even have a toehold in his life. If this saint would have drawn up daily to-do lists, he would have run out of ink. After eighty years, he accomplished his last task: he died and entered into a much-deserved eternal rest.

Philip calmly accepted that fact that we end our days by dying. Not even the God-man Jesus was exempt. Billionaires listed by Forbes, celebrities with stars on the Hollywood Walk of Fame, dictators, and kings all die. No matter how much we accomplish or accumulate, we all die. The knowledge of his inexorable fate did not put a damper on Philip's *joie de vivre*. He lived life to the fullest and brightened the world with spontaneous antics, demonstrating that holiness is not at all incompatible with fun and humor. He was not above being a fool for Christ. Imagine how the halls of heaven ring with laughter now as he entertains the other saints.

Joy is not a nicety but a necessity. Laughter, a ministry in itself, can bring peace and a feeling of wellbeing. In the spirit of Philip, let us fill our days with joy, confident that life on earth is worth living and that it is only the opening act for an indescribable life of bliss. Satan may have howled with wicked glee at the fall of the human race, but God had the last laugh when on Easter Sunday we were raised up again in the person of Jesus Christ.

RESPONSE

On a scale from one to ten, ranging from serious to lighthearted, where would you land? Do or say something to make someone laugh, even if it is silly, outrageous, or makes you look the fool.

St. Pio

Gesu, Maria.

Saint Pio of Pietrelcino

1887–1968 • Priest, Religious, Mystic • September 23

LIFE

The son of a farmer in Italy, the man who would one day be known as Padre Pio joined the Capuchin Franciscan Friars at the age of fifteen. Poor health kept him at home for six years after his ordination. In 1918, Padre Pio experienced the pains and then the bleeding of the stigmata. The wounds of Jesus that appeared on his hands and feet lasted for the rest of his life. Padre Pio spent much time in prayer and had a unique devotion to the guardian angels. His devout celebration of Mass and the sacrament of Penance attracted many people. Padre Pio loved the poor and established two hospitals.

LAST WORDS

Gesu, Maria.

REFLECTION: PRAYER

Engulfed in a terrible storm, a sea captain tried everything he knew to keep his ship afloat. As a last resort, he fell to his knees and prayed, "O God, I haven't bothered you for twenty years. Save us and I won't bother you for another twenty." Saint Pio, on the other hand, wouldn't have hesitated to fall to his knees. Prayer would have been his first response to any of life's storms.

Prayer is communicating with God, or as someone defined it, wasting time gracefully. In prayer we speak to God, listen to him, think about him, express our love for him, or simply rest in him, aware of his presence. Through prayer we nourish and deepen our relationship with God in the same way that we foster a relationship with a fellow human being. Prayer is as necessary for our spiritual life as is breathing for our physical life.

It's important to pray as you can, not as you can't, choosing from a smorgasbord of prayer forms ranging from the Our Father to contemplation. Many people today are drawn to meditating on God's word in Scripture, especially through *lectio divina*, or "holy reading." First, read a passage until a word or phrase grabs your attention. Mull over that word or phrase, pondering how it pertains to you until you experience the "aha moment." Motivated by that realization, respond with a short prayer. Then contemplate God, using no words but simply being aware of him in loving silence.

Why pray? First of all, we owe God—the almighty One and our Creator—the prayer of adoration. It is our destiny to spend eternity glorifying God with all the angels and saints. The prayer we offer in our life on earth is a rehearsal for heaven. Second, our thanks are due for all the good things God showers on us—everything we are, have, and experience. Third, after offending our loving Father and Redeemer, it is only right that we apologize and ask forgiveness. Finally, we can ask God for help for ourselves or others and be assured of a response. As Pio was fond of saying, "Pray, hope, and don't worry."

RESPONSE

What is your usual way of praying? Spend extra time in prayer on Sunday, the Lord's Day, and experiment with a form of prayer that is new to you.

Pope Saint Pius V

1504–1572 • Religious, Pope • April 30

LIFE

Pope Saint Pius V was born in Italy. As pope he wore the white habit of his Dominican order. A man of great holiness, he sent his coronation money to the needy and practiced penance. Despite ill health, he achieved a great deal, primarily carrying out the decisions of the Council of Trent. He examined Church finances, simplified the lifestyles of the hierarchy, held synods, began regular meetings for parish priests, and oversaw a new catechism, Roman Missal, and Divine Office. After victory over the Turks at the Battle of Lepanto was accredited to praying the rosary, Pope Pius V established what we now celebrate as the Feast of the Holy Rosary.

LAST WORDS

O Lord, increase my sufferings,
and also increase my patience!

REFLECTION: PATIENCE

"Give me patience, Lord, right now," is what we Americans, who do not like to waste a minute, might pray. We resent standing in line, sitting in front of the computer for a slow download, or being trapped behind a car going at or below the speed limit. We like fast food, instant coffee, and express mail. Pope Saint Pius V prayed for sufferings, aware of their value, but he also asked for patience, which is the virtue of enduring pain, discomfort, or inconveniences calmly. The root word of patience is the Latin *patiens*, meaning "suffering."

Patient people respond to trials with gentleness and constancy. They wait out life's storms without growing angry or irritable. Patience, or longsuffering, is counted among the fruits of the Holy Spirit. In other words, it is a sign that God is at work in us.

We are called to exercise patience when a person doesn't act the way we wish. At times we must be patient with ourselves, as when we break a resolution, struggle to master a new skill, or become ill. We also must be patient with God during the times we pray furiously and he seems to be on vacation. It takes patience to develop the difficult virtue of patience. The German priest Thomas à Kempis remarked that everyone recommends patience although few are willing to practice it. When we are patient, we are nothing less than Godlike. For God is "slow to anger" (Numbers 14:18) and very patient with us, his sometimes exasperating children.

RESPONSE

In what area of your life are you being called to exercise patience? Ask the Holy Spirit to grant you this grace.

Pope Saint Pius X

1835–1914 • Pope • August 21

LIFE

Pope Saint Pius X, born Giuseppe Sarto in Italy, was a parish priest for seventeen years. As pope, he allowed children to receive the Eucharist, promoted Bible study, and encouraged Catholics to be involved in politics. He taught that justice and charity would bring about peace, and he sponsored refugees with his own resources. In vain Pope Pius X worked to prevent World War I and avowed, "I would gladly give my life to save my poor children from this ghastly scourge." He died twenty-two days after the outbreak of the war. His last words were the motto he had chosen for his papacy.

LAST WORDS

To restore all things in Christ

Reflection: Promoting God's Kingdom

In 1999, the final restoration of the marvelous frescoes of the Sistine Chapel was revealed. Grime and candle smoke had been cleaned off and cracks filled in. Michelangelo's depiction of salvation history again shone forth in brilliant colors. Ever since the fall of our first parents in Paradise, the human race has been undergoing restoration. Original sin darkened the glory God first planned for us and shattered our friendship with him. Jesus, the carpenter from Nazareth, repaired the damage, but in many ways our lives still cry out for renewal.

We hear daily news reports about the evils that mar our beautiful world and our souls: human trafficking, pornography, racism, genocide, persecution, and war, to name a few. Many people are forsaking God, and family life is threatened. Christians are needed to make the world what it should be—to restore all things in Christ.

Popes and world leaders obviously have more clout when it comes to effecting change. But never doubt the impact a single person can make. As someone wisely commented, "If you think you're too small to make a difference, you have never been in bed with a mosquito." Imagine if every Christian took steps to eradicate evil in his or her sphere of influence. The world would more like Paradise, and the daily news would not be as disturbing. By promoting the good, peace, and justice, we make more real the kingdom of God, the pristine masterpiece that the Divine Artist originally intended.

Response

What facet of your life needs restoration? Do something practical to bring it more in line with God's vision for you.

Saint Polycarp

c. 60–155 • Bishop, Martyr • February 23

LIFE

Saint Polycarp, a disciple of Saint John the Apostle, became the bishop of Smyrna in what is now Turkey. During a persecution, he was seized and pressured to renounce his Christian faith. Polycarp replied, "For eighty-six years I have served him, and he has done me no wrong. How then can I blaspheme my Lord and Savior? Bring forth what you will." He was condemned to death by fire. When the flames miraculously failed to harm him, he was killed by the sword. The document *The Martyrdom of Saint Polycarp* is the earliest recorded account of a Christian martyr.

LAST WORDS

I bless you, that you have granted me this day and hour, that I may be numbered among the martyrs to share in the cup of your Christ and to rise to everlasting life, both of soul and body, in the immortality of the Holy Spirit. May I, today, be received among them before you, as a rich and acceptable sacrifice, as you, the God who lies not and is truth, has prepared beforehand, and shown forth, and fulfilled. For this reason, and for all else, I praise you, I bless you, I glorify you through....

Reflection: Sacrifices

The prayer recorded in the account of Saint Polycarp's martyrdom may not be his actual final words, but it expresses the ideal sentiments of a martyr. Praising God for your execution may seem incongruous—unless you have the eyes of faith. Polycarp viewed death as a share in the suffering of Christ, the suffering that reversed our fate and brought about eternal life. It is only natural, then, that Polycarp welcomed his fate.

Polycarp turned the surrender of his life into a sacrifice, a gift to God. The word *sacrifice* is derived from the Latin for "to make holy." We too can sacrifice ourselves to God when we pray the Morning Offering, giving God our prayers, works, joys, and sufferings. As a result, all of our hardships become infused with meaning. Sometimes life is an obstacle course, giving us one challenge after another. Our car breaks down, we get sick, someone steals from us, or we experience failure. Then there are the daily minor irritations. When we make the sacrifice, God can transform our trials into wellsprings of grace.

One day as I swept the chapel stairs, our chaplain came by and commented, "Offer every speck of dust for the poor souls." This may sound quaint to our modern ears, but it is based solidly on the Catholic belief in the communion of saints. Our prayers and sacrifices contribute to a treasury of grace that can be channeled to other members. So, as we offer up the moments of our lives to God, we can earmark them for a special intention, for example, for a friend who is facing surgery. Likewise, we benefit from the prayers and sacrifices of other Christians, including Polycarp, whose name appropriately means "much fruit."

Response

Who is praying and sacrificing for you right now? Make it a practice to offer hardships that spoil your tranquility for a relative or a friend in need.

Saint Rita of Cascia

1386–1457 • Widow, Religious • May 22

LIFE

Saint Rita, an Italian, was married to an abusive husband for eighteen years. When her husband was murdered in a family feud, she prayed that her two sons would not take revenge. After those sons died of illness, Rita reconciled the feuding families and became an Augustinian nun known for penance and powerful prayers. One day as she prayed before a crucifix, a wound appeared in her forehead, purportedly caused by a thorn from Christ's crown. She bore this form of stigmata for fifteen years. She spoke her last words to the nuns gathered around her.

LAST WORDS

*May God bless you
and may you always remain
in holy peace and love
with your beloved Spouse Jesus Christ.*

REFLECTION: THE MARRIAGE METAPHOR

Marriage imagery has been used to describe the relationship of Jesus to the Church, beginning with Jesus himself, who said, "The wedding guests cannot fast while the bridegroom is with them, can they?… The days will come when the bridegroom is taken away from them, and then they will fast on that day" (Mark 2:19-20). Marriage is a covenant between people who love each other, and ours is a covenant sealed with Christ's blood. The ideal marriage is lasting, weathering storms. Our bond with Christ is meant to endure forever. Marriage is also exclusive; no one is loved as dearly as one's spouse. Likewise, no one or no thing should come between Jesus and us. Our baptismal vows are as binding as marriage vows.

Already in the Old Testament, God spoke of his intimate relationship with his people in terms of marriage. He promised them, "I will take you for my wife forever; I will take you for my wife in righteousness and in justice, in steadfast love, and in mercy. I will take you for my wife in faithfulness; and you shall know the LORD" (Hosea 2:19-20). God also stated, "Your Maker is your husband" (Isaiah 54:5).

The marriage metaphor is applied in a particular way to women religious like Saint Rita, who are called brides of Christ and may wear a ring as a reminder of their "marriage" vows. Some saints, notably Saint Catherine of Siena, experienced a mystical marriage with Christ; her vision was complete with a ritual and ring, signifying a special grace of union with God.

Scripture describes our entrance into heaven at the end times in this manner: "For the marriage of the Lamb has come, and his bride has made herself ready" (Revelation 19:7). She is clothed "with fine linen, bright and pure" (Revelation 19:8). This heavenly bridal gown is handmade, woven of righteous deeds. Saint Paul wrote that we, the Church, are to be presented to Christ as a bride "in splendor, without a spot or wrinkle" (Ephesians 5:27). In other words, we are to be radiantly holy, loving God with all our heart as he loves us.

RESPONSE

Pray for perseverance for sisters and nuns. Ask God to plant in the heart of more women the desire to commit themselves to him as consecrated religious.

St. Rose
of Lima

SANTEE '08

Gesu, Maria.

Saint Rose of Lima

1586–1617 • Virgin, Third Order Dominican • August 23

LIFE

Saint Rose was born Isabel Flores y Oliva in Peru, but at her Confirmation she took the name Rose. As a young girl, she began a life of prayer, penance, and care for the sick and hungry. She enjoyed the privilege of daily Communion and spent hours before the Blessed Sacrament. To earn a living, Rose sold her needlework and home-grown flowers. Because her father forbade her to become a Dominican nun, she joined the Third Order of Saint Dominic, made a vow of virginity, and lived as a recluse in her room at home. Rose has the distinction of being the first canonized saint from the Americas.

LAST WORDS

Lord, increase my sufferings,
and with them increase your love in my heart.

Reflection: The Purposes of Suffering

Painkillers—narcotic and non-narcotic, over-the-counter and prescription—drive one of the largest businesses in the United States. While we look for relief from suffering, Saint Rose welcomed it and even pleaded for more. She shared Saint Paul's point of view: "Suffering produces endurance, and endurance produces character, and character produces hope, and hope does not disappoint us because God's love has been poured into our hearts through the Holy Spirit" (Romans 5:3-5).

Rose understood that, in addition to developing character, sufferings enable us to play an active role in the redemption of the world. That is why Saint Paul wrote, "I am now rejoicing in my sufferings for your sake, and in my flesh I am completing what is lacking in Christ's afflictions for the sake of his body, that is, the church" (Colossians 1:24). Was the suffering of Jesus insufficient to atone for all sin? Not at all. Rather we, who are Christ's body today, continue to bear suffering patiently and without bitterness as a witness to the world.

Suffering is also important because it is a prerequisite for personal salvation. Scripture explains that we are heirs of God with Christ "if, in fact, we suffer with him so that we may also be glorified with him" (Romans 8:17). As the saying goes, "No pain, no gain." Rose realized that suffering is eased when it is borne with love.

Response

Who do you know who is suffering mentally or physically? Share the Christian understanding of suffering and pray with them.

Saint Rose Philippine Duchesne

1769–1852 • Virgin, Religious • November 18

LIFE

Born in France, Saint Rose became a Visitation Sister, living with her community until it was closed during the French Revolution. She returned home and later joined the new Society of the Sacred Heart. Her dream of being a missionary in America came true when she was sent to Saint Louis, where she and her sisters opened the first free school west of the Mississippi. As their superior, Rose founded six convents. At age seventy-one, she asked to work with the Native Americans in Kansas. Unable to master their language, she simply prayed—so much that they gave her the name "Woman Who Always Prays." Rose lived her last ten years in prayer and penance in one of her order's convents in Missouri.

LAST WORDS

Jesus, Mary, Joseph,
I give you my heart, my soul, and my life—
oh, yes, my life, generously.

Reflection: Self-oblation

Catholic school students were taught to write J.M.J.—the initials for Jesus, Mary, and Joseph—on the top of their papers, dedicating their work to the Holy Family in the way that books, songs, and films are often dedicated to significant people. With her dying breath, Rose turned over the work of her entire life to Jesus, Mary, and Joseph. She offered it wholeheartedly, confirming both her consecration at Baptism and her consecration as a vowed woman religious.

We give God the gift of our life by surrendering to him all we are and all we possess—every atom of our being, every ounce of strength, every action and thought, and every success and failure. We are actually re-gifting—returning all the gifts we have received. By doing so, we make God, rather than self, the axis of the universe.

Belonging to God gives us a special dignity. We show that we belong to God not by sporting an "I belong to God" label or a tattoo. Rather, we show that we are his through our actions, by living as God wants us to live. Our self-donation occurs at every Mass. The bread and wine carried in the Offertory Procession are symbols of all we are and do. As we offer them to the Father, we offer ourselves—our whole life, just as Saint Rose offered hers.

Response

After the priest accepts the bread and wine, he prays as he raises the paten with the host. As he does so, realize that it is *you* he is offering to God along with the sacrifice of Jesus.

Saint Stephen

?–c. 36 • Deacon, First Martyr • December 26

LIFE

A Greek convert, Saint Stephen was one of the first seven deacons chosen to help the apostles with the distribution of food. He performed miracles in the name of Jesus and spoke well, but certain Jews had him falsely accused of blasphemy. As Stephen faced the council, his face had the look of an angel. After summarizing Jewish history, he bluntly stated that the Israelites had rejected the prophets and now they were rejecting God's Son. Naturally this angered his listeners. Then Stephen declared that he was seeing a vision of God and Jesus in heaven. When the council heard these words, they dragged Stephen outside and stoned him to death.

LAST WORDS

Lord Jesus, receive my spirit.
Lord, do not hold this sin against them.

Reflection: The Gift of Faith

In Luke's account of the crucifixion, Jesus commended his spirit to the Father and forgave his persecutors. In the Acts of the Apostles, which is also Luke's work, Saint Stephen echoed the dying words of Jesus, handing over his spirit not to the *Father* but to *Jesus*. Stephen did this because he accepted the truth that Jesus, a Jew, was the Son of God and the Lord of heaven and earth. This conviction prompted Stephen to become a Christian and then a deacon, a man chosen to be charity incarnate. Teaching that Jesus was Lord cost Stephen his life.

Faith in Jesus is a sheer gift. Why did the gentile Stephen come to believe in Jesus, while most Jewish leaders did not? Why do you believe Jesus is God? Today many factors threaten and test our faith. Living in a secular society, shocked by sins of some clergy members and puzzled by catastrophes, both man-made and natural, we may wonder at times whether Jesus really was a God-man and whether we can trust his promises.

When our faith is shaken, we can strengthen it by praying to the Trinity and reading Scripture. We can also shore it up by associating with others who exhibit a strong faith and by recalling saints like Stephen who were so convinced that Jesus is divine that they gave up their lives as testimony. At Stephen's death, the executioners' cloaks were laid at the feet of young Saul. Possibly Stephen's life and death helped earn the grace that changed Saul into Saint Paul.

Response

When we profess Jesus as our Lord, we do what pleases him. In particular, we serve him in the poor. Find a way to carry out the ministry of charity as would a deacon.

Saint Teresa of Avila

1515–1582 • Virgin, Religious, Doctor of the Church • October 15

LIFE

Born to a wealthy family in Spain, Saint Teresa joined the Carmelites at a time when the sisters in this community were lax in observing the rules. After eighteen years, she received the grace to love Jesus more deeply, leading to experiences of visions and ecstasy. Called to reform the Carmelites, she began founding convents for a strict order called Discalced (shoeless) Carmelites. Influenced by her idea, two friars aided her in establishing reformed monasteries for Carmelite men. One of them, John of the Cross, became Teresa's spiritual director and friend. Teresa opened sixteen convents and wrote the now-classic *The Interior Castle*, a book about mental prayer. She was the first woman named a Doctor of the Church.

LAST WORDS

O my Lord and my Spouse,
the hour that I have longed for has come.
It is time for us to meet each other.

REFLECTION: KNOWING JESUS

Richard Neave, a medical artist from England, and his research team used forensic anthropology to construct a likeness of a first-century Galilean Semite man. The image can be jarring, especially to those of us familiar with the Jesus of icons and the Shroud of Turin. Neave's work suggests that Jesus was swarthy and had a broad face, short dark hair, brown eyes, and a beard. Skeletons of Semitic men suggest that Jesus stood about 5'1" and weighed 110 pounds, the average size for people of his time. Of course, because Jewish law forbade images and because no contemporary of Jesus described his physical appearance, his image remains a question mark except in the visions of a few mystics.

We are drawn to Jesus, not by his striking good looks, but by his life, teachings, and works recorded in the gospels. Our personal spiritual encounters with him intensify this attraction. Without seeing Jesus with our eyes, we come to know him in his word, Sacred Scripture; under the forms of bread and wine; in one another; and as Saint Teresa of Calcutta pointed out, in the distressing guise of the poor. We both listen to and speak to him in prayer.

Like Saint Teresa of Avila, who devoted her entire life to Jesus, we look forward to that day when we will finally see our hidden friend face-to-face. In the meantime we can only imagine how his glorified body and his face appear. Judging from the account of the Transfiguration, he will be an awesome sight! Beholding him in the flesh for the first time will be the highpoint of our lives. No matter what Jesus looks like, as he gazes back at us, we surely will be overwhelmed by the love in his eyes.

RESPONSE

Reflect on meeting Jesus for the first time after your death. What will you say to him?

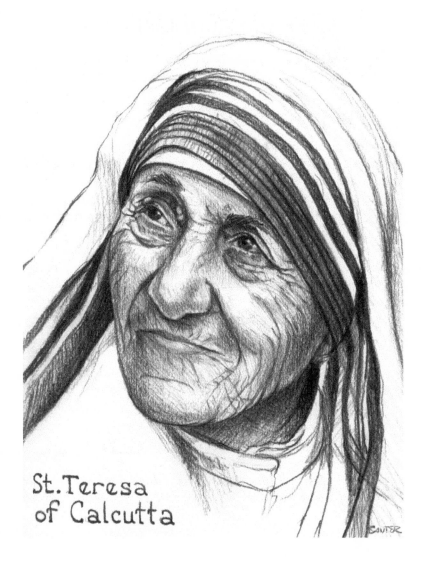

St. Teresa
of Calcutta

Jesus, I love you. Jesus, I love you.

Saint Teresa of Calcutta

1910–1997 • Religious, Founder • September 5

Life

Known the world over as Mother Teresa, this Albanian woman was regarded as a living saint because of her exceptional poverty and good works. As a child, she longed to be a missionary in India. At age eighteen she moved to Ireland in order to join the Sisters of Loreto. Two months later she sailed to India and became a teacher. In 1946, Teresa heard an interior call to leave the convent and help the poor by living with them. She obeyed, received medical training, and began the Missionaries of Charity and the Missionary Brothers of Charity. These orders serve the poorest of the poor, including lepers, the dying, and abandoned babies. In 1979, Mother Teresa was awarded the Nobel Peace Prize. She was canonized in 2016.

Last Words

Jesus, I love you. Jesus, I love you.

REFLECTION: ENDURING THE DARK NIGHT OF THE SOUL

A little boy couldn't fall asleep alone in the dark. His mother told him, "Don't be afraid. You know that God is with you." The boy replied, "Yes, but I want someone with a face." Although God is pure spirit, we sometimes can sense his presence and love. Speaking and listening to him in prayer fills us with peace and joy. Some saints had visions of Jesus, Mary, and other saints. Some went into ecstasies and experienced mystical espousals. Not Saint Teresa. She was not favored with such supernatural privileges. In fact, after Mother Teresa died, it was revealed that she had been without an awareness of God for almost fifty years.

True, Mother Teresa once heard God's voice, calling her to a new vocation. After that, except for one brief respite, God was silent. No one except her spiritual directors knew that behind her smile, she was in torment, suffering the absence of God. She felt as though God had abandoned her and at times questioned his very existence.

Other saints knew this trial of spiritual dryness. Saint John of the Cross called it the dark night of the soul. Despite this ordeal, Teresa accomplished extraordinary things for God and his poorest people. She accepted the cross that identified her with Jesus who, while dying, cried out, "My God, why have you abandoned me?" Teresa remained faithful, always yearning for God, devoting her life to him and his poor people, and loving him although she felt no love in return. She stands as an encouraging model for us on days when we find ourselves bereft of God's consolation.

RESPONSE

Say a prayer for anyone you know who may be undergoing the dark night of the soul. Ask that he or she may have the grace to persevere in their faith and love for God.

Saint Thérèse of the Child Jesus

1873–1897 • Virgin, Religious, Doctor of the Church • October 1

LIFE

Saint Thérèse, known as the Little Flower, was born in France, the youngest of nine children. After her mother died, she was raised by her aunt and sisters. She entered the Carmelite convent at Lisieux at the young age of fifteen in the footsteps of two of her sisters. Her path to sainthood followed her "Little Way," her spiritual practice of doing ordinary tasks extraordinarily well. Her autobiography, *The Story of a Soul*, reveals both her great love for God and her struggles. Because of her prayerful support of priests and missionaries, this cloistered nun was named the patroness of missionaries. As she lay dying of tuberculosis, Thérèse promised to let fall a shower of roses, to spend her heaven doing good on earth. Many people were attracted by her spirituality, and devotion to her spread quickly. Thérèse was declared a Doctor of the Church by Saint Pope John Paul II.

LAST WORDS

Oh, I love him. My God, I love you.

REFLECTION: LOVING GOD

The familiar passage in 1 Corinthians 13, sometimes called the Hymn to Love, lists attributes of love, such as "love is patient" and "love is kind." For a unique examination of conscience, substitute your name for "love" in all of these verses. How closely do these attributes describe you? If Saint Thérèse used this as an examen, Saint Paul's description would fit her to a T.

Thérèse once declared, "My vocation is love." Actually we are all called to that vocation: to be holy, in other words, to love. In her "Little Way," Thérèse carried out each chore, no matter how insignificant, to the best of her ability for the love of God. She transformed every little action, even picking up a pin, into an act of love. We might say she made her life a lovely valentine for God. She also manifested her love of God by loving others, God's children. She once made up her mind to love a nun she found disagreeable in every way. Thérèse was so successful in loving this person that one day the nun inquired, "What attracts you so much towards me? Every time you look at me, I see you smile."

Thérèse's "Little Way" led her to a huge reward. Now from heaven she continues to pour out love on others, granting requests of those who ask her for favors.

RESPONSE

Before tackling a major or minor task, take time to offer it to God as an act of love.

Saint Thomas Becket

1118–1170 • Bishop, Martyr • December 29

LIFE

Born in London, Saint Thomas Becket was chancellor of England for eight years until King Henry II made him Archbishop of Canterbury. As a Church leader, Thomas changed his somewhat worldly lifestyle. He incurred Henry's anger by opposing state control of the Church and took refuge in a French abbey for six years. On returning to England, Thomas discovered that Henry had subverted his authority as Archbishop of Canterbury by having his bishops crown his son king. When Thomas upheld the pope's decision to cut these bishops off from the Church, Henry exclaimed, "Will no one rid me of this troublesome priest?" Taking this as an order, Henry's knights killed Thomas in the cathedral as he was about to join the monks for Vespers.

LAST WORDS

For the name of Jesus
and for the defense of the Church,
I am ready to die.

REFLECTION: LIVING THE FAITH

Historian Arthur Schlesinger, Jr., called anti-Catholicism "the deepest bias in the history of the American people." Philip Jenkins, a professor and the author of a book on the subject referred to it as "the last acceptable prejudice." It is challenging to be a Catholic when our positions on vital issues are counter-cultural. Only the brave swim against the current. We may not risk being killed for our faith as Saint Thomas was, but living our faith can make us unpopular, invite scorn and ridicule, and block job advancement.

Potential repercussions may make us reluctant to go forth and preach the good news as Jesus commanded. We may be tempted to take the more comfortable and safer route: to remain quiet and do nothing. Saint Thomas was ready to die for Jesus and his Church. Are we ready to live for them? Are we willing to grow in our knowledge of the faith, to be identified as Catholic, to work for justice? Will we eschew the idols of vanity, arrogance, and pride? In his inimitable way, Pope Francis cautioned, "All of us have to strip ourselves of this worldliness." Or else, he continued, "we become pastry shop Christians, like beautiful cakes and sweet things but not real Christians."

Jesus warned, "Whoever denies me before others, I also will deny before my Father in heaven" (Matthew 10:33). The apostles who ran and hid when Jesus was arrested were just as culpable as Saint Peter, who openly disavowed his relationship with him. We may not be asked to take a stand against a king, but we must take up the equally as important and difficult task of showing and declaring our allegiance to Christ to our friends and neighbors. Our baptismal vows demand it.

RESPONSE

Take advantage of opportunities that come your way to share your Catholic faith.

St. Thomas More

I die the king's good servant but God's first.

Saint Thomas More

1478–1535 • Layman, Martyr • June 22

LIFE

After becoming chancellor of England, Saint Thomas More, an admired lawyer and devoted family man, refused to approve King Henry VIII's divorce. He also would not sign the document making the king head of the Catholic Church in England. After resigning his post, Thomas was imprisoned for more than a year in the Tower of London, standing firm when King Henry tried to persuade him to change his mind. At his beheading, Thomas retained his sense of humor. Moving his beard out of the way of the axe, he remarked, "This has not offended the king."

LAST WORDS

I die the king's good servant but God's first.

Reflection: Integrity

The film *A Man for All Seasons*, based on a play of the same title, garnered six Academy Awards. Its success in large part was due to its subject matter: the integrity of Saint Thomas More. The word *integrity* is derived from the Latin word for wholeness or perfection. Thomas strived to live as God intended us to live, that is, untainted by sin. He was a man who followed his conscience, preferring to serve God over any human being, including a king. Even the threat of death failed to move him. Resolute to the end, Thomas obeyed God in the manner of the prophets of old. And, like John the Baptist, who did not tacitly endorse King Herod's immorality, Thomas was beheaded.

Each of us is endowed with a conscience, a moral compass. It is defined as our reason, our ability to judge an act to be good or bad, and it is sometimes referred to as God's voice within us. If our conscience is formed correctly, it impels us to make the right decision. If we do not, it goads us like a sharp stone in our shoe. We can also muffle our conscience by ignoring it so that it no longer disturbs us.

The pressure to compromise our morals to please a friend, a loved one, or a boss can be intense. We might choose to be untrue to ourselves for fear of the consequences. Likewise, because we are social beings, we are inclined to go along with the crowd even when that crowd is wrong. In that case, we resemble lemmings that, according to popular myth, fall off a cliff and plunge into the sea *en masse*. By forsaking our principles, we might manage to escape ridicule, loneliness, or even natural death, but we risk eternal death. In the end we have to answer to God, who is not only King of England but the King of heaven and earth.

Response

Virtues are good habits that grow through repetition. Obey God in small ways in order to build up strength for a time when you might be called upon to obey in a serious matter.

Saint Vincent de Paul

1580–1660 • Priest, Founder • September 27

LIFE

After growing up on a farm in France, Saint Vincent was ordained to the priesthood. One day, while on a voyage, his ship was attacked and he was made a slave. After escaping to Rome and engaging in a year of study, he became chaplain to a noble Parisian family and lived a life of luxury. A holy man persuaded Vincent to turn his back on this lifestyle and serve the poor and sick instead. Vincent and the young men he gathered to join in this endeavor became Vincentian priests. Rich friends came to the aid of the Vincentians and so did the club of ladies organized by Vincent and Saint Louise de Marillac. These women, who collected food and funds for the poor, evolved into a religious community, the Daughters of Charity.

LAST WORDS

We have done what you commanded;
do now what you have promised.

REFLECTION: PROMISES

Johnny was talking in class again. "Johnny, didn't you promise to behave?" his teacher asked. "Yes," he replied. "And didn't I promise to punish you if you didn't?" the teacher added. "Yes, but since I broke my promise, you don't have to keep yours," the boy retorted.

Promises are so crucial to the fabric of society, to every relationship, that God safeguarded them in the eighth commandment. The Old Testament introduced us to the concept of covenant, a solemn promise made between God and an individual or a group. God promised Abraham a land, as many descendants as the stars, and blessings for all nations through one of those descendants. At Mount Sinai, the Israelites agreed to do everything God command-ed, and God promised to be their God. Although the Israelites re-peatedly broke their promises, God was ever faithful.

God's word is good. We can depend on it without fearing that God, the Rock, the immutable One, will change his mind. We can trust Jesus, the Son of God, to keep his promises. One colossal promise he made us was that anyone who believed in him would enjoy eternal life. (See John 6:40.) He gave this promise credibility by putting death to death, leaving behind an empty tomb.

Saint Vincent was bound to God by his baptismal promises in which he vowed to believe in God and to reject sin. He strove to keep these promises and, furthermore, he cooperated when God called him first to become a priest and then to serve the poor. Vin-cent died knowing that he had kept his side of the bargain. He had every right to call on God to be true to his word and show him into heaven.

RESPONSE

If you are not faithful to your baptismal promises in some way, re-commit yourself to them.

Saint Vincent Ferrar

c. 1350–1419 • Priest, Religious • April 5

LIFE

A zealous Dominican priest, Saint Vincent lived at a time when three men claimed to be pope. He worked hard to see that the rightful pope was recognized and, as commanded in a vision of Jesus, Saint Dominic, and Saint Francis, preached Christ to the world. After one of these powerful sermons, the false pope Benedict XIII had to flee. Vincent spent his life fasting, working miracles, and preaching throughout Europe to large crowds, many of whom joined the Church or renewed their commitment to their faith. When he was dying, he asked to have the story of the Lord's passion read to him. A small portion of what Vincent might have heard is included here from the account in the Gospel of Luke.

LAST WORDS

It was now about noon, and darkness came over the whole land until three in the afternoon, while the sun's light failed; and the curtain of the temple was torn in two. Then Jesus, crying with a loud voice, said, "Father, into your hands I commend my spirit."

Reflection: The Passion and Death of Jesus

When I was a young sister, an older sister encouraged me to pray the Stations of the Cross, saying, "It will help you bear suffering when it enters your life." Saint Vincent apparently was aware of this piece of wisdom. As he endured the death agony, he desired to focus his attention on the sufferings of Jesus. Although he was innocence itself, Jesus freely chose to undergo pain and death. By doing so, he redeemed the world and imbued our lives and our sufferings with meaning. The cross became the logo for Christianity.

Jesus was not blessed with an easy or a happy death. After a night of torture and mockery, he was brutally nailed to a cross. Crucifixion was the cruelest means of execution, reserved only for slaves and rebels. Jesus could have come down from the cross if he had wished. He could have saved himself. After all, he was God. But love kept him there. Jesus persevered not only through physical pain, but the psychological pain of knowing that his death was agonizing for his mother. He also suffered the human grief of being deserted by friends and, if we take his dying words literally, he may have felt abandoned by God, echoing Jesus' words from the cross: "O God, my God, why have you abandoned me?"

Author J. R. R. Tolkien coined the word *eucatastrophe* to describe a tragedy that turns into a happy ending. The passion story that moves from Jesus' suffering and death to his rising from the dead is arguably the quintessential example of eucatrastrophe. Vincent believed that the bitter sacrifice of Jesus made his own life of sacrifice and his own death worthwhile. Thanks to Jesus, he could anticipate his own resurrection.

Response

Pray the Stations of the Cross by using a booklet or by simply meditating on each station. Or thoughtfully read an account of the passion of Jesus from one of the gospels.

Saint Wenceslaus

c. 907–929 • Martyr • September 28

LIFE

Saint Wenceslaus was Duke of Bohemia. After his father died in battle, his non-Christian mother assumed power. Wenceslaus was educated as a Christian by his grandmother, Ludmilla, whom his mother later had killed. After Wenceslaus assumed the throne, he reconciled with his mother and ended the persecution of Christians, but he and his brother, Boleslaus, had a disagreement. One day when Wenceslaus was on his way to Mass, Boleslaus struck him on the head with a sword. As the two struggled, friends of Boleslaus killed Wenceslaus. Boleslaus repented and was a good successor of Wenceslaus. In fact Boleslaus' daughter became a nun and a son was educated to become a priest. The saint is immortalized in the Christmas carol "Good King Wenceslaus."

LAST WORDS

Brother, may God forgive you.

Reflection: Jesus as Model of Forgiveness

Except for "I love you," "I forgive you" are probably the three most important words we can say. They are also the most difficult, often getting stuck in our throat. Jesus demands that his followers practice forgiveness, which is a primary ingredient in bringing about God's kingdom of peace.

Over and over the gospels show Jesus hammering home the need to forgive by his example. He forgave the crafty and despised tax collector Zacchaeus, the adulterous woman whom self-righteous religious leaders were determined to kill, the repentant woman whose tears fell on his feet, Dismas justly crucified next to him, the people responsible for his death, Peter the betrayer, and other cowardly apostles. Some surmise that Jesus even forgave the traitorous Judas and spared him hell. Today Jesus offers us, his brothers and sisters, forgiveness through the Sacrament of Penance in which we actually hear his representative declare, "I forgive you."

Forgiveness was also a frequent refrain in Jesus' teachings. He said, "Love your enemies and pray for those who persecute you" (Matthew 5:44) and "Forgive, if you have anything against anyone; so that your Father in heaven may also forgive you your trespasses" (Mark 11:25). A few of his parables were about forgiveness. Jesus taught that we must forgive not only superficially but from our heart, the core of our being.

In his words and actions, Saint Wenceslaus proved to be an apt student of the gospels. He knew that "I forgive you" is another way of saying "I love you." And he knew that loving not only fulfills the greatest commandment but has power to work miracles, like the repentance of Boleslaus.

Response

Clashing opinions, misunderstandings, and hurts, intentional or not, tear down good relationships. Rebuilding them is hard work demanding courage, humility, and patience. Reach out to someone among your relatives or friends who is estranged from you.

Appendix A

Select Prayers

Litany of the Precious Blood

Lord, have mercy.   Lord, have mercy.
Christ, have mercy.   Christ, have mercy.
Lord, have mercy.   Lord, have mercy.

(Respond "have mercy on us" to each of the following invocations.)

God our Father in heaven
God the Son, Redeemer of the world
God the Holy Spirit
Holy Trinity, one God

(Respond "be our salvation" to each of the following invocations.)

Blood of Christ, only Son of the Father
Blood of Christ, incarnate Word
Blood of Christ, of the new and eternal covenant
Blood of Christ, that spilled to the ground
Blood of Christ, that flowed at the scourging
Blood of Christ, dripping from the thorns
Blood of Christ, shed on the cross
Blood of Christ, the price of our redemption
Blood of Christ, our only claim to pardon
Blood of Christ, our blessing cup
Blood of Christ, in which we are washed
Blood of Christ, torrent of mercy
Blood of Christ, that overcomes evil
Blood of Christ, strength of the martyrs
Blood of Christ, endurance of the saints
Blood of Christ, that makes the barren fruitful
Blood of Christ, protection of the threatened

Blood of Christ, comfort of the weary
Blood of Christ, solace of the mourner
Blood of Christ, hope of the repentant
Blood of Christ, consolation of the dying
Blood of Christ, our peace and refreshment
Blood of Christ, our pledge of life
Blood of Christ, by which we pass to glory
Blood of Christ, most worthy of honor

(Respond "have mercy on us" to the following three invocations.)

Lamb of God, you take away the sins of the world
Lamb of God, you take away the sins of the world
Lamb of God, you take away the sins of the world

Lord, you redeemed us by your blood.
You have made us a kingdom to serve our God.

Let us pray.
Father, by the blood of your Son you have set us free and saved us from death. Continue your work of love within us, that by constantly celebrating the mystery of our salvation we may reach the eternal life it promises. We ask this through Christ our Lord. Amen.

Holy Trinity, Whom I Adore

O my God, Trinity whom I adore, let me entirely forget myself that I may abide in you, still and peaceful as if my soul were already in eternity; let nothing disturb my peace nor separate me from you, O my unchanging God, but that each moment may take me further into the depths of your mystery! Pacify my soul! Make it your heaven, your beloved home and place of your repose; let me never leave you there alone, but may I be ever attentive, ever alert in my faith, ever adoring and all given up to your creative action.

O my beloved Christ, crucified for love, would that I might be for you a spouse of your heart! I would anoint you with glory, I would love you—even unto death! Yet I sense my frailty and ask you to adorn me with yourself; identify my soul with all the movements of your soul, submerge me, overwhelm me, substitute yourself in me that my life may become but a reflection of your life. Come into me as Adorer, Redeemer, and Savior.

O Eternal Word, Word of my God, would that I might spend my life listening to you, would that I might be fully receptive to learn all from you; in all darkness, all loneliness, all weakness, may I ever keep my eyes fixed on you and abide under your great light; O my Beloved Star, fascinate me so that I may never be able to leave your radiance.

O Consuming Fire, Spirit of Love, descend into my soul and make all in me as an incarnation of the Word, that I may be to him a super-added humanity wherein he renews his mystery; and you, O Father, bestow yourself and bend down to your little creature, seeing in her only your beloved Son in whom you are well pleased.

O my "Three," my All, my Beatitude, Infinite Solitude, Immensity in whom I lose myself, I give myself to you as a prey to be consumed; enclose yourself in me that I may be absorbed in you so as to contemplate in your light the abyss of your splendor!

Litany of the Holy Name of Jesus

Lord, have mercy. Lord, have mercy.
Christ, have mercy. Christ, have mercy.
Lord, have mercy. Lord, have mercy.

(Respond "have mercy on us" to each of the following invocations.)

God our Father in heaven
God the Son,
Redeemer of the world
God the Holy Spirit
Holy Trinity, one God
Jesus, Son of the living God
Jesus, splendor of the Father
Jesus, brightness of everlasting light
Jesus, king of glory
Jesus, dawn of justice
Jesus, Son of the Virgin Mary
Jesus, worthy of our love
Jesus, worthy of our wonder
Jesus, mighty God
Jesus, father of the world to come
Jesus, prince of peace
Jesus, all-powerful
Jesus, pattern of patience
Jesus, model of obedience
Jesus, gentle and humble of heart
Jesus, lover of chastity
Jesus, lover of us all
Jesus, God of peace
Jesus, author of life
Jesus, model of goodness
Jesus, seeker of souls
Jesus, our God
Jesus, our refuge
Jesus, father of the poor
Jesus, treasure of the faithful
Jesus, Good Shepherd
Jesus, the true light

Jesus, eternal wisdom
Jesus, infinite goodness
Jesus, our way and our life
Jesus, joy of angels
Jesus, king of patriarchs
Jesus, teacher of apostles
Jesus, master of evangelists
Jesus, courage of martyrs
Jesus, light of confessors
Jesus, purity of virgins
Jesus, crown of all saints

(Respond "Jesus, save your people" to each of the following invocations.)

Lord, be merciful
From all evil
From every sin
From the snares of the devil
From your anger
From the spirit of infidelity
From everlasting death
From neglect of your Holy Spirit
By the mystery of your incarnation
By your birth
By your childhood
By your hidden life
By your public ministry
By your agony and crucifixion
By your abandonment
By your grief and sorrow
By your death and burial
By your rising to new life
By your return in glory to the Father
By your gift of the holy Eucharist
By your joy and glory

Christ, hear us   Christ, hear us
Lord Jesus, hear our prayer   Lord Jesus, hear our prayer

(Respond "have mercy on us" to each of the following invocations.)

Lamb of God, you take away the sins of the world
Lamb of God, you take away the sins of the world
Lamb of God, you take away the sins of the world

Let us pray.
Lord, may we who honor the holy name of Jesus enjoy his friendship in this life and be filled with eternal joy in the kingdom where he lives and reigns for ever and ever. Amen.

ACT OF LOVE

O my God, I love you above all things, with my whole heart and soul, because you are all good and worthy of all love. I love my neighbor as myself for the love of you. I forgive all who have injured me and ask pardon of all whom I have injured. Amen.

MORNING OFFERIING

O Jesus, through the Immaculate Heart of Mary, I offer you my prayers, works, joys, and sufferings of this day for all the intentions of your Sacred Heart, in union with the Holy Sacrifice of the Mass throughout the world, for the salvation of souls, the reparation of sins, the reunion of all Christians, and in particular for the intentions of the Holy Father this month. Amen.

Appendix B
Patron Saints

Agatha: Nurses, miners, jewelers, Sicily, bell founders, breast diseases, protector against fires, earthquakes, famine, thunderstorms, volcanoes

Aloysius Gonzaga: Youth, students in Jesuit colleges

André Bessette: Family caretakers in Canada

Andrew Kim Taegon: Korean clergy

Angela Merici: Sickness, disabled people, orphans

Anselm: Theologians

Anthony of Egypt: Gravediggers, domestic animals, butchers, skin diseases

Anthony of Padua: Lost articles, childless women, the poor, harvests, travelers, horses and donkeys, Portugal, Brazil

Antonius of Florence: Italy, the Philippines

Bede the Venerable: English writers and historians

Benildus: Teachers

Bernadette: Illness, France, shepherds, against poverty, people mocked for their faith

Boniface: Germania, England, tailors, brewers

Bruno: Germany, Calabria, monastic fraternities, possessed people

Catherine of Siena: Italy, fire prevention

Charles Borromeo: Catechists, seminarians, stomach trouble

Charles Lwanga: African Catholic Action, youth

Clare: Television

Cyprian: North Africa, Algeria

David: Wales, vegetarians

Dismas: Prisoners, funeral directors, repentant thieves

Dominic: Astronomers, Dominican Republic, falsely accused people

Dominic Savio: Young boys, choirboys, falsely accused people, juvenile delinquents

Elizabeth Ann Seton: Catholic schools; Maryland; Shreveport, Louisiana

Elizabeth of Hungary: Catholic charities, Franciscan Third Order, bakers, nurses, hospitals, brides, widows, dying children, exiles, homeless

Elizabeth of Portugal: Coimbra, Portugal; Diocese of San Cristóbal de la Laguna

Elizabeth of the Trinity: Sick people, orphans, against illness

Frances of Rome: Widows, motorists, Benedictine Oblates

Francis of Assisi: Italy, ecologists, Catholic Action, animals, Cub Scouts, merchants

Francis de Sales: Authors, editors, journalists, Catholic press, the deaf

Francis Xavier: Missions, Australia, India, Pakistan

Frederick: The deaf

Gabriel Possenti: Students, youth, clerics, seminarians, Abruzzi region of Italy

Gemma Galgani: Students, pharmacists, paratroopers, parachutists, loss of parents, those suffering back pain or headaches, those tempted to impurity

Gertrude the Great: West Indies

Gregory VII, Pope: Diocese of Sovana, other popes named Gregory

Hugh of Grenoble: Grenoble, France; headaches

Ignatius of Loyola: Retreats, soldiers, educators

Jeanne Jugan: The destitute elderly

Jerome Emiliani: Orphans, abandoned children

Joan of Arc: France, French soldiers, martyrs, captives, prisoners, people ridiculed for their piety

John Baptist de le Salle: Teachers, principals

John Bosco: Editors, publishers, young people, magicians, juvenile delinquents

John Chrysostom: Preachers, public speakers, Constantinople, epilepsy, education

John of the Cross: Diocesan priests, contemplatives, mystics, Spanish poets

John Neumann: Catholic education

John XXIII, Pope: Papal delegates, Patriarchy of Venice, Christian unity, the Italian army

John Paul II, Pope: Archdiocese of Krakow, World Youth Day, young Catholics, families

Joseph Cupertino: Aviation, astronauts, mental disabilities, test-taking, students

Josephine Bahkita: Sudan

Julie Billiart: Catechists, poverty, bodily ills, disease

Justin Martyr: Philosophers

Kateri Tekakwitha: Native Americans, ecologists, people in exile, people ridiculed for their piety

Lawrence: Rome, cooks, the poor, comedians, librarians, students, miners, firefighters

Lawrence Ruiz: The Philippines, Filipinos, the poor, separated families

Louis de Montfort: Preachers

Margaret Clitherow: Businesswomen, converts, martyrs

Margaret Mary Alacoque: Those suffering with polio, devotees of the Sacred Heart, loss of parents

Margaret of Scotland: Scotland, Anglo-Scottish relations

Maria Goretti: Youth, teenage girls, victims of rape, crime victims

Martin of Tours: Soldiers, France, horses and riders, alcoholics, hotel-keepers, beggars, geese, winegrowers

Mary Magdalene de Pazzi: Against bodily ills, against sexual temptation, the sick, Naples

Monica: Parents, mothers, difficult marriages, disappointing children, victims of adultery or unfaithfulness, victims of verbal abuse, conversion of relatives

Paschal Baylon: Eucharistic congresses and associations

Paul Miki: Japan

Perpetua: Mothers, expectant mothers, ranchers, butchers

Peter of Alcantara: Brazil, Eucharistic adoration

Peter Chanel: Oceania

Peter Verona: Guaynabo, Puerto Rico; midwives

Philip Neri: Rome, US Special Forces, laughter, humor, joy

Pio of Pietrelcino: Civil defense volunteers, adolescents, stress relief, January blues

Pius V, Pope: Valetta, Malta; Bosco Marengo and Pietrelcina, Italy

Pius X, Pope: Pilgrims, first communicants, several dioceses

Polycarp: Earache, dysentery

Rita of Cascia: Impossible causes, sickness, wounds, marital problems, abuse, mothers

Rose of Lima: Florists, gardeners, Peru, Central and South America, the Philippines, India

Rose Philippine Duchesne: Perseverance and adversity, Diocese of Springfield-Cape Girardeau

Stephen: Deacons; bricklayers; stonemasons; altar servers; casket makers; headaches; horses; Owensboro, Kentucky

Teresa of Avila: Headaches, Spain, bodily ills, loss of parents, people in need of grace, people in religious orders, people ridiculed for their piety

Teresa of Calcutta: World Youth Day; Missionaries of Charity

Thérèse of Lisieux: Missions, florists and gardeners, France, Russia, HIV/AIDS sufferers, loss of parents, tuberculosis, Alaska, aviators

Thomas Becket: Secular clergy; Exeter College, Oxford; Portsmouth; Arbroath Abbey

Thomas More: Lawyers, politicians, statesmen, adopted children, large families, difficult marriages, widowers, stepparents; civil servants, Diocese of Arlington, Diocese of Pensacola-Tallahassee

Vincent de Paul: Charitable societies, hospitals, prisoners, Madagascar, Saint Vincent de Paul Societies; volunteers, horses, leprosy, lost articles

Vincent Ferrer: Builders, construction workers, plumbers

Wenceslaus: Bohemia, Prague, Czech Republic, brewers

Index of Saints
Arranged by Name

Index of Saints
Arranged by Feast Day

Index of Reflections
Arranged by Title

About the Author

Mary Kathleen Glavich, a Sister of Notre Dame and noted religious educator, is the author of more than eighty books on faith formation, including the award-winning books *The Catholic Companion to Jesus* and *The Confirmed Catholic's Companion.* She has also written *The Heartbeat of Faith: 59 Poems, Fingerplays, and Prayers; Why Is Jesus in the Microwave? Funny Stories from Catholic Classrooms; Totally Catholic: A Catechism for Kids and Their Parents and Teachers;* and a novel, *The Fisherman's Wife: The Gospel According to St. Peter's Spouse.* Mary Kathleen also gives talks and retreats. She blogs at www.kathleenglavich.org.

About the Illustrator

Christopher Santer has made drawings of more than one hundred different saints, bringing them to life with a realness that gives you the sense that you could encounter these holy people on the street. Santer has exhibited works in galleries and museums across the country, including Los Angeles, Seattle, Minneapolis, Boston, and Miami. Prints of his work, available at pacemstudio.com, have been shipped to all fifty states and nine foreign countries. He is a recipient of the 2004 McKnight Foundation Fellowship (Minneapolis, MN) and his work has been featured in the bi-monthly publication, *New American Paintings* (#47). He earned his M.F.A. from Ohio University and his B.F.A. from the University of Dayton. Santer is the Fine Arts Department Chair at Providence Academy in Plymouth, Minnesota, and continues to work out of his studio in St. Paul, Minnesota. His full body of work can be seen on his website: christophersanter.com.